REPRODUCING RACISM

Reproducing Racism

How Everyday Choices Lock In White Advantage

Daria Roithmayr

NEW YORK UNIVERSITY PRESS

New York and London

NEW YORK UNIVERSITY PRESS
New York and London
www.nyupress.org

References to Internet websites (URLs) were accurate at the time of writing.
Neither the author nor New York University Press is responsible for URLs that
may have expired or changed since the manuscript was prepared.

LIBRARY OF CONGRESS CATALOGING-IN-PUBLICATION DATA
Roithmayr, Daria.
Reproducing Racism : How Everyday Choices Lock In White Advantage / Daria Roithmayr.
pages cm
Includes bibliographical references and index.
ISBN 978-0-8147-7712-1 (hardback)
1. Racism—United States. 2. Whites—United States—Economic conditions. 3. Whites—
United States—Social conditions. 4. Minorities—United States—Economic conditions.
5. Minorities—United States—Social conditions. 6. Racism—United States. 7. Race
discrimination—United States. 8. United States—Race relations. I. Title.
E184.A1R4467 2014
305.800973—dc23
2013029823

New York University Press books are printed on acid-free paper,
and their binding materials are chosen for strength and durability.
We strive to use environmentally responsible suppliers and materials
to the greatest extent possible in publishing our books.

Manufactured in the United States of America
10 9 8 7 6 5 4 3 2 1
Also available as an ebook

For my family,
who has always accepted me
just as I am

CONTENTS

ACKNOWLEDGMENTS

The reason I got into academia in the first place was the freedom to think, teach, and write on the issues I care most about. As important if not moreso has been the opportunity to collaborate, and this book was the highlight of my professional life in that regard.

Richard Delgado first came to me, now many years ago, with the idea that I write a book, though he had wanted me to focus on what would become a very small part of the book—the argument that institutional rules of distribution, like merit, were defined by the folks who occupied the institution at the beginning. I had bigger ambitions, however, and though Richard warned me that I might be biting off too large a piece to finish quickly, I forged ahead. Finish quickly I did not.

Mary Dudziak was invaluable in helping me to craft a book proposal that worked, and my agent Jacquelyn Hackett took the proposal the rest of the way. Debbie Gershenowitz, my editor at NYU, sold me by not only understanding my original vision but by pushing me to do more than I had planned, to my great benefit.

Special mention goes to the USC Law and Humanities reading group, with David Cruz, Ariela Gross, Clyde Spillenger, Hilary Schor, and Nomi Stolzenberg participating in the critical and careful reads for which this group is famous.

Faculties at many law schools helped to refine the ideas, among them Georgetown University Law Center, UCLA, NYU, American, University of Pretoria, University of Cape Town, University of Witswatersrand, and the Center for Civil Society at the University of Kwa-Zulu Natal. Many a presentation at Lat-Crit and Critical Race Theory conferences was taken up with a piece of the book, and questions from the audiences there were among the finest.

My critical readers hold a special place in my heart; they gave me the greatest gift in sharing with me their hardest questions and their most supportive skepticism. Among them I would list Lani Guinier, Richard Ford, Loïc Wacquant, Ian Haney-López, Ariela Gross, Patrick Bond, Jonathan Jansen, Guy Charles, Shmuel Leshem, Scott Altman, and Matt Spitzer. I don't know if they will appreciate the designation of critical, though I hope they understand how valuable I found their critique to be. They are my secret weapon.

Another special mention goes to Katie Waitman and Hilary Habib, who coordinated production and double-checking of the manuscript with all the brilliance of a well-executed military campaign. Katie read the entire manuscript in two days, and provided me with wonderful edits any professional editor would be proud to call her own.

Finally, my family and dear friends served as my sounding boards, my source of moral support, my cheering section, and my incentive to hurry and finish ("you mean you still haven't published it yet?"). They are too many to mention (and I am desperately afraid of leaving someone out). All the same, my brother Carlos deserves special mention: he was my ideal crossover reader, and his comments were superb. Learning (or relearning) to write for a nontechnical audience was a painful process, and Carlos helped me to translate what had been overly technical jargon into something more comprehensible. I'll never go back to the technical writing, now that I've crossed over. I am grateful to him and to the people I've listed, and others too numerous to mention.

Introduction

At the beginning of Barack Obama's second term, the image of a black man against the backdrop of grand marble and the stately appointments of the Oval Office seems quite routine and unremarkable. Photographs and footage show a man very much at home in the White House. Even at the beginning of his first term, Obama moved easily and comfortably through the halls of power, in contrast to other relative newcomers to insider Washington, like Jimmy Carter for instance.

Contemplating Obama's reelection, we might all too easily forget that not too far from the White House, just east of the Anacostia River in fact, sits the Capitol's historic ghetto. Abandoned houses sit sentry on either side of the street. Barbed wire surrounds the neighborhood's few parking lots. Buildings are boarded up, and few streets show any signs of economic activity. Libraries, public schools, and health clinics are nowhere to be seen. Anacostia residents are almost all African American. It wasn't always that way. White flight and urban decay changed the face of the area.

As the 2012 election results are reviewed, many commentators have begun to ask again whether Obama's presidency has heralded an important turning point in the country's conversation about race. Commentators on both the right and left insist that we are all "postracial" now, meaning that race no longer marks a salient social division in the country's psyche. "Racial polarization used to be a dominating force in our politics—but we're now a different, and better, country," declared liberal economist Paul Krugman.[1] "When it comes to race," wrote conservative scholar John McWhorter in 2009, "Obama's first year has shown us again and again that race does not matter in America the way it used to. We've come more than a mere long way—we're almost there."[2]

To be sure, racial polarization doesn't dominate presidential elections the way that it once used to. And scholars will debate for some time to come what exactly Obama's presidency signals about voter attitudes on race. But is McWhorter right? Are we almost there?

The short answer is no, not by a long shot, at least, not if the numbers are any indication. Indeed, on almost every measure of well-being, the numbers tell a grim story. Racial disparities persist, long after the end of Jim Crow and legal segregation, and the gap between white and non-white shows no sign of disappearing.

Consider wealth, for instance. The wealth gap between white and black families has actually quadrupled—that's right, increased by fourfold—over the course of the last generation. Research shows that the gap in wealth between black and white families increased from $20,000 to $75,000 between 1984 and 2007. The black middle class turns out to be not all that middle-class when wealth serves as the relevant measure. Indeed, black families defined as high-income still have far less wealth than white families defined as middle-income. A whopping $56,000 in wealth separates a high-income black family (earning more than $50,000 in income in 1984) from a middle-class white family (earning $30,000 in the same year).[3] Just to be clear, the middle-income white family owns more wealth than the high-income black family. The potential for confusion is illuminating.

At the bottom of the spectrum, poverty falls disproportionately hard on people of color, much as it has over the last few decades. Poverty rates themselves have risen and fallen over the last sixty years. But the gap between races has remained huge, with Latino and black rates of poverty registering between two and half and four times the rates for whites.[4] Likewise, homeownership rates have demonstrated dramatic racial differences, with 26- and 30-point differences in rates of ownership between whites on the one hand and blacks and Latinos on the other, respectively.[5]

Not surprisingly, the one-two punch of the real-estate market and the economic recession has hit people of color at the bottom particularly hard. Latinos were the most affected by the crash, and wealth gaps have doubled in the aftermath. Latino wealth fell 66 percent between 2005 and 2009, compared to just 16 percent for whites.[6] White to black wealth ratios went from eleven to one to nineteen to one, and Latino ratios almost doubled, from seven to one to fifteen to one. Currently, wealth gaps are the highest they have been during the last thirty years.[7]

How much money are we talking about with regard to those wealth gaps? As of 2009, blacks had a median net worth (excluding homes) of $2,200, the lowest recorded for the last thirty years, where whites' median wealth registered at $97,900, 44.5 times the median wealth for blacks.[8] Over the last three decades, blacks have consistently held a small fraction—roughly 20 percent—of white wealth.[9] Researchers' estimates may vary somewhat, but all agree that wealth gaps are dramatic and quite persistent.

What about education? Conventional wisdom teaches that education is the great equalizer across race and class difference. But race and class differences themselves blunt the force of the great equalizer. Schools have largely resegregated along racial and class lines. Poor and working-class black and Latino students attend schools that are grossly under-funded, relative to white schools. When research takes into account men who have been incarcerated, the statistics show that young Latino and black men drop out at roughly twice the rate that young white men do (20.2 percent and 23.4 percent, respectively, versus 10.9 percent). The longer view is more optimistic for some groups—dropout rates have fallen over time for white and Latino young men. But rates for black young men have remained unchanged over the last few decades.[10]

Most dramatic and depressing are the racial gaps in incarceration and infant mortality. Those gaps have exploded over the last two decades. The most famous statistic is shocking. As of 2006, one in nine black men between the ages of twenty and thirty-four are now in the custody of the state or federal government.[11] Over the age of eighteen, the incarceration rate is one in fifteen and one in thirty-six for black and Latino men respectively, compared to only one in 106 for white men of the same age.[12] Of course, these rates reflect that more people overall are being incarcerated—general rates increased fivefold after the year 1975.[13] But by and large, owing in large part to the war on drugs, race and incarceration have become intertwined. People in the US carceral system are dramatically and disproportionately black and brown men.[14]

Surely the most heartbreaking gap of all is the persistent difference in infant mortality. The rate for black mothers is 2.4 times the rate for white women, and like other gaps, the disparity in infant mortality has not changed for decades.[15] These gaps showed up as early as one hundred years ago, when researchers first started collecting data. No one studying the issue predicts that these gaps will diminish, let alone disappear.

Far from being postracial, then, race continues to matter. When we focus less on presidential politics and more on material differences in well-being, we are not "almost there." We are not even close.

This book is about why racial inequality persists. It offers a new explanation for why we continue to see significant racial differences—in labor, housing, education, and wealth, in health care, political power and now incarceration—decade after decade. In particular, this book argues that racial inequality reproduces itself automatically from generation to generation, in the everyday choices that people make about their lives. Choices like whether to refer a friend (or the friend of a friend) for a job or whether to give one's child help with college tuition turn out to play a central role in reproducing racial gaps. Even if all people everywhere in the US were to stop intentionally discriminating tomorrow, those racial gaps would still persist, because those gaps are produced by the everyday decisions that structure our social, political, and economic interactions. Put another way, racial inequality may now have become "locked in."

Light on this subject comes from a most unexpected place—innovative work by a group of scholars on a phenomenon called "lock-in." Economists like Brian Arthur have developed the "lock-in model" to explain why an early lead for one technology can sometimes persist for extended periods even when the technology faces competition from a superior alternative.[16] The lock-in model focuses on the way that competitive advantage can begin to automatically reproduce itself over time until the advantage eventually becomes insurmountable or, in a phrase, locked in.

A story about Microsoft will help to illustrate the key features of the lock-in model. In the mid-1990s, the US government charged that Microsoft had acted illegally to gain an unfair monopoly in the operating systems market, in violation of US antitrust law.[17] According to the allegations, Microsoft engaged in a range of very bad (and illegal) behavior that pushed computer manufacturers to buy Microsoft's operating system, Windows. For example, the complaint noted that manufacturer contracts with Microsoft were unusually long-term contracts, which limited the manufacturer's ability to switch to a competitor. In addition, Microsoft charged manufacturers a licensing fee per computer produced, whether or not the computer had Windows loaded. If manufacturers wanted to load another operating system onto the computer, they had to pay twice—once to Microsoft, and once to the developer of the alternate operating system.

As the judge in the litigation noted, Microsoft's bad behavior went on to trigger a "positive feedback loop" in the operating systems market.[18] This feedback loop connected software authors and consumers. Consumers wanted to buy an operating system with the widest range of software available. In turn, software authors wanted to write software for the operating system with the most customers. Because of this loop, every increase in consumers triggered a future increase in software authors. Of course, every increase in software authors produced an increase in consumers and the company's small early advantage snowballed.[19]

Ultimately, the company's market advantage became locked in. Other competitors could not possibly overcome the software company's advantage.[20] Notably, Microsoft's monopoly advantage lasted long after the company stopped engaging in anticompetitive behavior.

This book will argue that white economic advantage has become institutionally locked in, in much the same way as Microsoft's monopoly advantage did. At the turn of the century and well into the twentieth century, whites worked to drive out their nonwhite economic competitors to gain an unfair advantage early in the game. Much like a predatory monopolist, whites formed racial cartels during slavery and Jim Crow to gain monopoly access to key markets. Homeowners' associations worked together with real estate boards to keep blacks out of housing markets. School boards worked together with local growers to keep Mexicans out of public schools. Working-class farmers worked together with elite planters to disfranchise blacks and eliminate their political power. These racial cartels used many of the same kind of anticompetitive strategies—economic boycotts and violence, for example—to unfairly drive their competitors out of the market.

This unfair advantage, acquired early in our nation's history, has now become self-reinforcing and cumulative. A number of institutional feedback loops parlay earlier advantage into continuing advantage. For example, a white person's decision to refer a friend for a job can work to reproduce the anticompetitive advantage that whites had earlier gained during Jim Crow and slavery. This is because social networks work to transmit earlier advantage and disadvantage to subsequent generations. Blacks and Latinos earn lower wages than whites in large part because the people in their social networks who will refer them for jobs are people who earn lower wages. Because the existing underemployed people in a network add new people who are more likely to be underemployed, the network is self-reproducing.

Likewise, gaps in wealth persist partly because of decisions about whether to give the next generation help in paying college tuition. Black and Latino families can't afford to send their kids to college or give them a down payment on a house. Each generation serves as the foundation for the next generation and so racial disadvantage reproduces itself, in the absence of significant class mobility. As we will see, research has traced the genesis of this self-reinforcing cycle to slavery and Jim Crow.

In the same way that disadvantage has become self-reinforcing, so too advantage has now become locked in. Whites have been able to build their wealth on the shoulders of earlier generations, who gained early wealth by driving blacks and Latinos and some Asian groups out of key markets. White families who owned slaves and unfairly profited from labor union exclusion of black workers have been able to pass down the benefit of that unfair wealth and wage advantage to their children. White families have used that wealth to pay for the next generation's college expenses or the down payment on the purchase of a house—both activities which in turn have earned the next generation even more wealth.

Thus, past inequality has paved the way in each new generation for continuing inequality. Advantage has become self-reinforcing, and so has disadvantage. As the Billie Holliday song puts it, "Them that's got shall get, and them that's not shall lose." This self-reinforcing system of distribution of resources and opportunities has been operating for hundreds of years, built on the foundations of slavery and Jim Crow. White advantage may now be impossible to overcome, absent some kind of significant government intervention to level the playing field.

The lock-in story deviates from many of the standard explanations about why racial inequality persists. As Chapter 1 describes, conventional theory explains persistent discrimination in three basic ways. Some scholars argue that people of color have embraced maladaptive cultures that keep them poor and jobless. Others have pointed to structural reasons—the migration of unskilled jobs overseas, the mismatch between work and residential location—to explain disparities in jobs, wealth and housing. Still others have pointed to persistent racism by whites—persistent preferences and beliefs in stereotypes, sometimes unconscious and hard to get at, other times statistical and borne out by the facts.

But the lock-in story of racial disparity highlights a number of things about racial inequality that conventional explanations obscure. First, the lock-in model highlights the profits that whites earned from racial exclusion during Jim Crow. Economics scholars have always assumed that racism would die out because discriminating was too costly. On the contrary, the lock-in model demonstrates that racism can pay off, and did so handsomely during Jim Crow. Chapters 2 and 3 describe the profit-maximizing behavior of Jim Crow "racial cartels"—homeowners' associations, labor unions, political parties, school districts, and other groups that worked to generate monopoly profits by excluding competitors. By coordinating to keep the neighborhood pure, white homeowners' associations were able to keep for themselves the best houses, in the best neighborhoods, with the wealthiest neighbors. By excluding black and brown children from public schools, whites monopolized the best public education for themselves. By dividing the labor market into two racially identifiable segments, white unions earned the highest wages, in the most prestigious jobs. In the South, whites had a monopoly lock on political power for decades. As these chapters illustrate, during the era of Jim Crow, discrimination paid off quite well.

Second, the lock-in model helps us to understand the dynamics that now connect the historical discrimination of Jim Crow to modern racial gaps. Chapters 4 through 9 describe the key mechanism—the institutional feedback loops—that automatically translated whites' early advantage into white continuing advantage. Chapter 4 illustrates the institutional relationships that connect the wealth that whites acquired during Jim Crow and slavery to modern wealth differences, as early wealth begets later wealth. Chapters 5, 6, and 7 explore similar dynamic loops in workplaces and neighborhoods, where structural advantages in whom you know and where you live have become automatically self-reinforcing over time.

Public financing plays a significant role in some of these feedback loops. As Chapter 8 describes, white neighborhoods are wealthier because they create concentrated pockets of people with wealth, which generates more public school funding than in neighborhoods of color. And of course, good public school funding produces in turn students who are more likely to acquire wealth and earn a high income, and move into wealthy white neighborhoods. Early unfair success breeds later unfair success.

Saying that racial inequality persists is not to say that racial arrangements have not changed. Of course those arrangements have evolved over time. But as we'll see, even when arrangements have evolved, they've done so in a way that further disadvantages communities of color. Chapter 8 explores, for example, the way in which black members of the middle class have over the last several decades moved into the suburbs, and the wealthiest of the poor have moved out of the ghetto. But the flight of these groups from major metropolitan cities has left behind a hyperghetto at the city's center with more poverty and joblessness than before. Mass incarceration and dramatic cuts in social assistance programs have speeded up this trend, and are important measures of well-being in their own right.

Chapter 9 argues that the lock-in model of racial inequality usefully reframes our understanding of persistent racial gaps. Where conventional models focus on intentional discrimination, the lock-in model focuses on self-reinforcing structural processes like social networks and family wealth distribution. The lock-in model emphasizes both the unfairness of early anticompetitive conduct and the need for significant government "antitrust" intervention to dismantle white monopoly on advantage.

Won't things improve over time? Not likely. We may be stuck with racial inequality indefinitely, absent some significant government intervention. As Chapter 10 shows, the cost of switching to a system that reduces racial disparity—in technical parlance, the "switching costs"—may be too high for people to pay voluntarily. For example, the cost in urban assistance dollars to bring whites back to a hyperghetto like the urban core of Detroit may be prohibitive. In addition, were such a move to be successful, it would inevitably cause the neighborhood to tip toward gentrification and displace low-income residents of color. Owing to the arrow of time, policy makers might not be able to undo residential segregation. We may have come too far down the road to switch to a system that reduces significant racial gaps. If we can't figure out how to restructure the way that our institutions distribute advantage and disadvantage, inequality likely is here to stay.

What can we do to dismantle locked in racial inequality? Given the nature of feedback loops, three avenues are open to us, as Chapter 10 explores in more detail. First, we can try to dismantle the feedback loops themselves. We can decouple funding for local schools from the wealth of the surrounding community, as many states have done. We can push employers to hire through formal mechanisms rather than by word of mouth. But in many cases, these feedback loops are so deeply embedded in the capitalist structural arrangements that characterize American life that dismantling them seems quite unlikely.

Alternatively, we can modify feedback loops to be more inclusive. For example, we could allow word-of-mouth hiring if employers solicit social networks that connect people of color to each other. Or we could permit employers to use informal social networks to hire only if they already had some critical mass of employees of color in place. Finally, we could push to generate parallel feedback loops for people of color. For example, policy makers could adopt a children's trust fund that targeted children from poor families of color to receive funds at birth, to be retrieved for housing or educational expenses.

At the end of the day, however, the lock-in story is far more of a description of how we got ourselves to where we are than a set of easy policy prescriptions designed to diminish those gaps. As is true for most models, however, the model helps to generate productive brainstorming about appropriate policy interventions by illuminating the core dynamics that explain persistent racial inequality.

Before we proceed, it is worth emphasizing that the lock-in model describes a process that is now technically race-neutral. Everyday choices that have little overt connection to race structure much of our racial landscape. Families pass down wealth to their children on the basis of family connection. Friends recommend each other for jobs because that's what friends do for people in their networks. Workplaces hire by word of mouth because it is cheaper and faster than advertising through more expensive channels. One might argue that the lock-in model is based on class or at the very least structural differences that inhere in a democratic, capitalist system.

But issues of class are, in the US, issues of race. This is true particularly when it comes to the poorest of the poor. Owing to our country's history, these processes have become inextricably linked to race. Owing to discrimination, those families who can afford to pass down wealth for college educations and housing down payments tend to be disproportionately white. The same goes for networks that are able to refer high-paying jobs in lucrative occupations. Set against the backdrop of Jim Crow and slavery, institutional feedback loops reproduce racial disparity even as they reinforce the ordinary structural differences that we take for granted. And in the absence of government intervention, race will continue to matter in many of the same ways it has mattered during the country's history, long after electing a president who is black—or Latino or Asian for that matter—becomes a regular event.

1

The More Things Change, the More They Stay the Same

Some (Incomplete and Unsatisfying)
Explanations for Persistent Inequality

In the mid-1990s, scholars Richard J. Herrnstein and Charles Murray published *The Bell Curve*, a provocative best-selling book about human intelligence. At the center of the book, the authors argued that the divide between highly intelligent people ("the cognitive elite") and the unintelligent was widening dramatically, because opportunities and resources were increasingly distributed on the basis of merit rather than class or social status. Noting that unintelligent people were reproducing at a faster rate than intelligent people, the authors went on to recommend that government intervene to reverse that trend for the sake of general welfare.

Most controversially, the authors argued that racial differences in IQ were traceable at least in part to genetic differences. More precisely, the authors deemed it "highly likely" that genes at least had something to do with racial differences in IQ scores, particularly with regard to differences between blacks and whites. To be sure, Herrnstein and Murray said they remained "resolutely agnostic" on the question of how much influence genetic deficits might play relative to the environment. At the same time, the book pushed pretty hard on the claim that black–white gaps could be traced to IQ differences, and that IQ differences in turn were genetic in part.[1]

Reaction to the book was both swift and critical. Readers didn't bother to parse the subtleties of the book's language, nor did they take much note of the authors' resolute agnosticism. Most famously, anthropologist Stephen Jay Gould forcefully denounced the book as less a scientific treatise than a manifesto of ideology, and he listed multiple ways in which the science behind the argument was quite weak or failed altogether.[2] One critic pointed out research indicating that scores for students of color appear to depend on what the test takers were told about how the test results would be used.[3] Other critics pointed out that the analysis ignored or underestimated the effect on IQ of education, class, and inheritance.

Herrnstein and Murray certainly were not the first scholars to use genes to explain persistent racial gaps. At various stages in our intellectual history, biologists and anthropologists have argued, amazingly enough, that the shape of the skull and brain size, and the genes for those traits, explained racial disparities. But many academics had thought that those kinds of genetic explanations were now off the table, so thoroughly had the early theories been discredited. In the end, much of the scientific community agreed that the book was riddled with mathematical errors, bad reasoning, and mis-citation of sources.[4] And of course, more than a few scholars accused the authors of racism.[5]

Over the last half-century, scholars have come up with a very wide range of explanations for persistent racial gaps. In this chapter, we will investigate the most commonly offered theories. As we will discover, each field has its own take on the subject, and the diversity of explanations is quite remarkable. Economists suggest that market imperfections cause whites to statistically discriminate. Biologists have proposed that genes play a role, though culture is the more likely culprit for some these days. And a growing number of scholars argue that the way we structure our social arrangements is responsible. As we will see, many of these explanations have seemed quite promising—but none of them has proved wholly satisfying, for reasons that will be become clearer as we go along.

Economic Explanations

First, consider the economists' explanations. According to the most popular explanation offered by economic theory, racial gaps persist because people for whatever reason have a taste or preference for discrimination, and imperfect market competition cannot drive those preferences out.[6] Say for example that employers harbor an irrational prejudice against Latinos. Employers might well refuse to hire Latino workers because they don't want to associate with them, and might even be willing to pay some price to accommodate that preference. Likewise, employers might discriminate not because of their own tastes but because other workers and customers might have such tastes.

Economists like Gary Becker have suggested that market forces will drum out this racism. In a perfectly competitive market, those employers, workers, and customers who have a taste for discrimination and are willing to pay to accommodate that taste will be outcompeted by those who don't have such tastes. This is because those tastes are expensive, competitively speaking—discriminating employers, workers, and customers will have to pay a cost to accommodate their tastes for exclusion.[7] For example, employers who don't want to hire Latino or black workers likely will have to pay higher wages to white workers because they will be hiring from a smaller pool.

In perfect market competition, market players are perfectly rational and all transactions go off without a hitch. Under those conditions, discriminating employers will eventually be replaced by nondiscriminating employers, who won't have to pay higher wages because they are willing to draw from the wider pool. Because nondiscriminating firms can operate more cheaply than discriminating firms, the market will favor nondiscriminators.

But as economists point out, perfect competition does not always exist outside theoretical models. For example, those markets in which people of color are not a big enough percentage of the population to let nondiscriminating employers easily fill slots with minorities could allow employers to indulge their taste for exclusion. Whether the market will drive out discriminating firms depends on a range of empirical factors: the degree of competition in the market, the demographics of the labor market, and other factors such as those described above. The takeaway point from this theory, then, is that racial gaps might persist because people still have a taste for exclusion, and competitive forces can't drive out people's taste for discrimination for a number of reasons.[8]

Another group of theories involve so-called rational discrimination. The taste-based explanations described above are agnostic about the source of people's tastes or preferences. In contrast, statistical discrimination models explain preferences to exclude as based on so-called rational generalizations about race. These models start with the presumption that employers frequently don't have perfect information about whether a worker is productive. Sometimes, for example, because white employers are more well-connected to other white workers through social networks, they have better information about white workers and less perfect information about workers of color.[9]

As a result, employers engage in stereotype. They may try to infer a worker's productivity by generalizing on the basis of easily observed traits like race or gender. Sometimes employers generalize on the basis of actually observed, real differences in productivity—for example, they generalize that black workers have less education (which is true owing to historic discrimination). Sometimes employers just imagine differences where they don't exist.

But in either case, those generalizations can become self-fulfilling. In particular, they may trigger minority decisions about whether to invest in becoming productive, which in turn fulfill the stereotype. If employers hire fewer workers of color because they generalize about their education levels, for example, those workers in turn will rationally invest less in the education, skills, and training. Why bother investing if you don't get a full return? As a result, even imagined differences can become real. Whether on the basis of stereotype or some observed correlation between race and education, if employers think that workers are less productive, they will in fact become less productive.[10]

What other explanations do economists offer for persistent racial gaps? Some theorists suggest that monopoly might be responsible for racial inequality (an idea on which this book builds). If an employer had a monopoly over the product market, then the firm would be able to determine wages without having to worry about being undercut by competitors. Likewise, in a "monopsonist" market (where one buyer dominates the market), if a firm (or group of colluding firms) were the only employer in the labor market, it could control wages and discriminate without threat of competition.

But in both these cases, the employers would have to be willing to surrender profits in the short run to maintain the monopoly in the long run. In the case of monopoly, for example, cooperating members could make much more by breaking the monopoly agreement. Economists find the notion that employers would surrender profits to be implausible. Moreover, most economists agree that *modern* markets are not characterized by monopoly or monopsony, and that the empirical support for such models is missing.[11] As we will see later, monopoly may well be part of the explanation for persistent inequality, but not in the way these models describe.

Biology and Social Science Explanations

We shall now say a word or two more about biologists and their genes-based explanations. Genetic explanations have long been a favorite of biologists at the turn of the century and conservative theorists in more modern times. Scholars like anthropologist Stephen Jay Gould have explored the darker days of our intellectual history, in which scholars argued that blacks and "Mongoloids" were inferior because of their physiological or genetic characteristics. Some so-called experts in "craniometry," for example, suggested that people of color possessed lower

IQs because their brains were smaller.[12] But as time passed, most if not all of these ideas were thoroughly discredited as scientifically unsupported, although the ideas did reappear in modified and more sophisticated form from time to time, as was true in *The Bell Curve*.[13]

For scholars in social science, in contrast, continuing intentional discrimination seems like the most intuitively appealing explanation for persistent racial gaps. But the research is pretty clear that American citizens don't harbor bias at nearly the levels they did during Jim Crow. Study after study documents that racial bias (at least the conscious kind) has gone down over the last forty years.[14] In light of that research, could continuing discrimination really explain the kinds of persistent racial gaps that we still see?

Possibly. Consider recent evidence in the context of jobs and housing. In several studies, researchers sent resumes with equivalent credentials to employers using names that identified the senders as black (for example, Jamal and Lakisha) or as white (Brad and Emily). Employers invited back for interviews those "job candidates" with white names 50 percent more often than they called back equally qualified black applicants.

Were they generalizing on the basis of race? Maybe they assumed that black-named applicants had a poorer skill set, even though the resume listed equivalent credentials. But the design of the study made that unlikely. Putting better credentials on the candidates' resumes improved the callback rate for white-named applicants, but not for black-named applicants.[15]

More likely, employers were stereotyping on the basis of names. They may have assumed that applicants with black-sounding names were apt to identify strongly with their racial identity or embrace a distinctively black culture. And of course they made no such assumptions about white-named applicants. Although researchers could not pinpoint the reason for different callback rates between black and white candidates, the study suggests that continuing discrimination might well be partly to blame for persistent racial gaps in jobs.

We see the strongest evidence of continuing discrimination in housing markets. As with the job candidates, researchers in housing discrimination often send in undercover "testers" to see whether real estate brokers and housing lenders will treat clients differently because of their race. Testers of different races are given identical credentials and housing interests, and are trained to follow the same script in their opening interactions with brokers and lenders.

The research shows consistently that blacks and Latinos have very different experiences when looking for a house than do whites. Black and brown testers are typically offered less information about housing, given fewer opportunities to see units, and get less help with financing. In addition, real estate agents steer black testers to property in neighborhoods that they don't show to whites. Likewise, Latino testers get less help with mortgage financing than do white testers.[16]

Some scholars theorize that continuing intentional discrimination might be cyclical. We might see it more when economic times are tough, and general inequality rises in all races. In these circumstances, competition for higher income jobs increases, and intentional discrimination increases because race is an easy difference to use in discriminating anti-competitively.[17] Likewise, psychologists have argued that whites might perceive certain events—affirmative action or the election of a black president, for example—as a threat to the material and status interests of whites as a group, and such perceived threats might motivate continuing intentional discrimination.[18]

One recent and quite compelling theory is subconscious bias. Some psychologists argue that racial gaps persist because people subconsciously hold stereotypical beliefs about others based on race, or subconscious associations between someone's racial category and their propensity for violence, for example.

At Harvard, Mazharin Banaji and her colleagues have designed a research instrument called the Implicit Association Test (IAT), which measures the strength of people's implicit racial biases. In the laboratory, computers measure the speed with which research subjects respond when they are asked to perform categorizing tasks. Initially, subjects are asked to categorize names—Lakisha, Jamal, Juan, Marta, Emily, Scott—or photographs of faces as belonging to particular racial categories.

Experimenters then ask subjects to engage in two categorizing tasks that associate race with pleasant or unpleasant emotion. First, they are asked to use one hand to respond to things that are unpleasant (say, that are violent) and also to black names or photos. They are asked to use the other hand to respond both to things that are pleasant and to white names or pictures. The categorizing task then is reversed, pairing violence with white names or photos and nonviolence with black names or photos.

A significant percentage of subjects tend to respond more quickly on the task that associates race with stereotypically pleasant or unpleasant associations—white with nonviolence, black with violence, for example. Researchers read the difference in response times as indicating implicit bias in favor of one group or the other, depending on the direction of the differences, or as neutral. The results are quite astonishing. Over 75 percent of self-identified whites and Asians demonstrate a bias in favor of whites against blacks. Even black test takers typically demonstrate an unconscious bias in favor of whites.[19]

Some scholars have questioned whether the implicit bias test measures anything other than people's familiarity or cultural knowledge of stereotypes. Alternatively, the test might just measure the greater salience of one racial identity—say black—in the category of race.[20] Raising more serious questions, critics also point out that IAT scores appear to vary when the same person takes the test under different circumstances.

Others question whether implicit bias affects decision making that is less split-second and more deliberative.[21] Police officers may have to make split-second decisions based on race, for example, if they have to decide whether the object a black suspect is pulling out of his pocket is his ID or a gun. But how relevant is implicit bias in longer, more deliberative decisions like those in which employers engage when deciding whom to hire?[22]

On this question, evidence is accumulating that IAT scores correlate to more deliberative behavior. IAT scores predict, for example, the way in which a prospective employer will assess a person's resume quality. In 2008, researchers in Sweden sent employers matched resumes with

Muslim-sounding names. This time, researchers followed up with the employers and administered an IAT. Perhaps not surprisingly, those employers who were less likely to call back a candidate with Muslim-sounding names scored higher on an IAT designed to measure preferences for or against Muslims.[23] In conclusion, even if researchers are not clear on what the IAT measures or how it relates to deliberative decision making, most scientists agree that the IAT measures something important that relates to continuing discrimination.

Culture and Its Connection to Structure

Let's now look at culture, one of the more popular explanations for persistent inequality. The argument that culture explains persistent racial gaps in well-being has a long intellectual history, worth reviewing at some length. Anthropologist Oscar Lewis first made the now-infamous argument that a "culture of poverty" explained persistent gaps. Explaining the status of the "slum dwellers of Mexico City," Lewis argued that they shared a subculture of poverty—practices like high divorce rates, early initiation into sex, abandonment of wives and children—with American blacks, who suffered the added disadvantage of racial discrimination. In Lewis's view, a culture of poverty was, like other cultural practices, "a way of life" that could be "passed down from generation to generation along family lines."[24]

In the mid-1960s, Senator Daniel Patrick Moynihan suggested that poverty persisted among American blacks because of a shift in the social fabric in the ghetto. Moynihan traced poverty to the fact that "the Negro family in the urban ghettos is crumbling," and the "fabric of conventional social relationships has all but disintegrated."[25] Moynihan issued a highly controversial report outlining the basic features of the culture of the "underclass." To be sure, the report stressed unemployment and underemployment as key causes, but those ideas were pretty much ignored in the heated discussion that followed the report's publication.

Critics of Moynihan's culture of poverty argument raised several points. First, they noted that culture is very hard to define, and a so-called subculture of poverty even more difficult to define with any precision. In the same vein, some of the literature defined the so-called culture of poverty in ways that seemed strange—evidence of the culture of poverty included purely factual indicators of poverty such as being unemployed, for example. Second, critics noted that researchers had a difficult time proving that such cultural practices are passed down from parent to child, when children also grow up in many of the same situational circumstances—unemployment, substandard schooling—as do their parents.[26]

Third, critics argued that many of the so-called pathological practices described by experts were in fact rational responses to poverty. Take for example the common choice by families of color to insulate themselves and their family members from outside networks and institutions. Sociologist William Julius Wilson has pointed out that for people who live in violent neighborhoods, being isolated makes a great deal of sense.[27] Far from being pathological, the practice is quite rational, even as it also deprives the family of potentially positive network connections.

Though the culture explanation fell out of fashion in the 1970s, it never entirely disappeared from the discourse around race. As the culture wars of the 1980s heated up, social scientists like Thomas Sowell and Abigail and Stephan Thernstrom argued that the racial gap in performance between whites and Latinos might be explained at least in part by cultural factors—for example, Latinos' limited education and their "propensity to work in unskilled jobs that don't require a knowledge of English."[28] Other scholars have pointed to the fact that West Indian blacks have succeeded economically to a greater degree than "native" black Americans, even though they are phenotypically indistinct.[29]

So what should we make of the culture argument? Is culture really the reason that people of color remain persistently poor when it comes to wealth, housing, health, political participation, and the rest? One way of answering this question is to say, as sociologist Wilson does, that the so-called cultural deficits can be more usefully understood as rational, adaptive responses to bad structural conditions.

First, let's define some key terms. When we refer to "structural conditions," we mean to include processes or environmental conditions that slot people into particular social positions, roles and networks. So structure includes things like residential segregation, unemployment, and the mismatch in geographic location between jobs and people's residences (which slots people into the position of unemployed). "Cultural practices," by contrast, might include a set of community-shared values, goals, and practices—things like collectively shared attitudes toward law enforcement, or in another example, the practice in some communities of female-headed kinship networks in which single-mother households band together in groups to share child care and other resources.

In Wilson's framework, structure shapes culture, and culture in turn shapes and contributes to structure. So for example, in neighborhoods that have many black and brown men in prison, combining female-headed households in resource networks makes a lot of sense. Of course, these "cultural practices" might also contribute to continued joblessness and poverty, if women become cut off from the relatively greater wealth (again owing to discrimination) resources that men (or at least white men) typically can access.[30]

At worst, then, the culture story is just plain wrong. At best, a story about culture that does not also discuss structure is radically incomplete. As this book will argue, the best explanations assert that culture and structure reflect and reproduce each other in a positive feedback loop that moves from culture to structure and back again.

We will end our review of other explanations by looking at the scholarship that first suggested that persistent racial gaps might be traced to feedback loops, though they weren't called that yet. In very early theoretical work back in the late 1970s, economist Glenn Loury offered a simple but powerful model to explain the persistence of racial poverty. In his model, group membership (in groups defined by race and class) affected a person's ability to acquire skills to earn an income, and, in turn, a person's race and wealth contributed to and shaped the race and class background of the group.[31]

Analogizing his theoretical model to the real world, Loury pointed out that residentially segregated neighborhoods produce underfunded schools, and parents with poorly connected social networks decreased a child's chances of getting a job. In particular, children from those neigh-borhoods or those parental networks are less likely to get (or have to pay more to get) the training to do skilled work. Accordingly, each genera-tion suffered the deprivations of the prior generation and reproduced them for the next generation.[32]

The argument in this book for lock-in draws heavily on Loury's early theoretical work on self-reinforcing phenomena, and similar work by complex systems theorists. The following chapters discuss four separate kinds of feedback loops—family networks, in which parents affect the wealth of their children; social networks, in which friends and cowork-ers affect each other's jobs chances; neighborhood networks, in which neighbors' collective wealth affect a neighbor child's education; and institutional networks, in which selection processes early on affect the job chances of future generations. We will explore the argument that, when considered all together, these feedback loops have locked racial inequality into place.

2

Cheating at the Starting Line

How White Racial Cartels Gained an Early
Unfair Advantage during Jim Crow

On a cold winter morning in Memphis, in January of 1919, a committee of four white switchmen marched into the office of one Edward
Bodamer, superintendent of the Yazoo and Mississippi Valley Railroad.
The switchmen were there, they said, to discuss a demand by the area
yard workers: fire all black workers, or they would strike. Bodamer
threw the switchmen out of his office, warning them as they left that a
strike would be illegal. Ignoring the warning, dozens of switchmen and
yardmen walked off the job in protest.[1]

Over the next five days, the strike spread like wildfire. Work at surrounding railroads and yards ground to a halt, shutting down the
region's transportation network and crippling the railroad's operations.
At its peak, the strike united over 650 white switchmen in racial solidar-
ity, shutting down transportation in the countless small towns that lined
the railroad in Tennessee, Mississippi, and Illinois. At the end of the

fifth day, the switchmen called a halt to the walkout, but only after the railroad had promised investigation by government mediators. For the time being, the black workers remained.[2]

A year later, the white switchmen were back in Bodamer's office. This time, they had additional firepower, having gotten the backing of the Brotherhood of Railroad Trainmen, one of the "Big Four" railroad brotherhoods. Unable to risk another damaging strike, Bodamer and the railroad caved to the switchmen's demands, and fired almost all of the company's black workers. At the committee's insistence, the railroad also adopted racially restrictive contracts that changed seniority systems and entrance requirements, and limited the number of black workers for particular positions.[3]

What was behind this strike? Why had white workers so suddenly demanded that the railroad evict its black workers? After all, black workers had been around the railroad for a while, working as trainmen and switchmen since the 1870s. Although white switchmen had occasionally complained in the past, they had not taken much action against either the railroads or black workers. What had changed?

In a word, the economy. Historian Eric Arnesen argues that the postwar economic uncertainty over jobs triggered the Memphis strike and fueled other strikes just like it. As the economy disintegrated after the war, workers faced a labor market in such wild disarray that labor officials could barely track the job market from week to week, let alone make longer-term forecasts.[4]

In addition, the wartime economy had cost white workers their positions of privilege. Out of necessity during the war, the railroad had abandoned its conventional practice of awarding jobs on the basis of race. To accommodate wartime labor shortages, a number of black workers had been slotted into historically white positions, and a few whites occupied historically black slots when the occasion demanded it.[5]

As soldiers came home from the war, however, railroads had to choose whether to go back to the practice of assigning jobs by race. Some railroads quickly shifted back to race-conscious assignments, while others abandoned tracking race and status altogether, a move that would come to cost them dearly.[6]

Following standard economic theory, we could easily describe the Memphis wildcat strike as an irrational preference for exclusion that would eventually be eliminated by market forces. Indulging this preference would have been costly for the railroad—it would have had to pay more for white workers not just because they were a limited pool, but also because, as unionized employees, they earned higher wages. In addition, by excluding black workers, white union members were giving up the opportunity to vastly increase their numbers, and correspondingly their strength, in their labor struggles against employers. Black workers could have supplied (and did eventually come to supply) an important addition to the ranks. Because discrimination cost unions and railroads in terms of competitive advantage, racism should have died out quickly, and if it didn't, imperfect market competition is to blame. Or so the story goes.[7]

But we could tell another story to explain the Memphis strike: a story in which whites' collective action was more profitable than it was costly. In this story, whites formed "racial cartels" to sidestep market competition and to earn higher wages than their black counterparts. In this story, the cost of discriminating was less than the material benefit to workers. Far from costing them, discrimination paid off, by earning striking workers higher wages.[8]

How did white workers earn higher wages from discriminating? Classic collective action explains these wages as a sort of monopoly profit. By forming a union that excluded black workers and by pushing employers to hire whites only, white railroad workers could drive up wages relative to their black and brown counterparts.

Employers also profited from discrimination in their fight against unions. By dividing the labor market in two, railroads maintained a ready-made stable of black strikebreakers perpetually on call to undercut the power of the white union. For railroad and workers alike, then, discrimination was win-win. And those benefits came at the expense of black workers, in the same way that cartels displace the costs of their profits onto someone else.

This chapter suggests that we can better understand the nature of Jim Crow discrimination if we think of it as cartel conduct. A cartel story focuses on the material benefits to collective action that monopolize benefits for one group at the expense of another. Collective discrimination earns its keep in the form of higher wages, better housing, higher property values, and greater political power.

Before we redescribe the worst of our racial history using a cartel framework, we should remember why investigating history is important in explaining modern racial gaps. Why isn't the past long over and done with? What is the link between historical segregation during Jim Crow and contemporary outcomes?

To see the importance of history, we will take an unexpected detour into probability theory, to look at something that mathematicians call the Polya urn model. In a Polya urn model experiment, researchers fill an urn with two balls, one red and one white. The experimenter draws a single ball from the urn, and then replaces it together with an additional ball of the same color as the ball she originally drew. If the draw produces a red ball, that ball goes back into the urn, together with another red ball. Same goes for white. The experimenter continues drawing and replacing for an infinite number of times.

In a typical set of draws, the percentage of red and white balls will fluctuate wildly in the first few draws. But at some key threshold point in the drawing process, as the urn continues to fill, the percentage of reds and whites settles at a particular proportion, and remains very stable for all later draws. Amazingly, later events don't change the final percentages in any appreciable way.

As mathematicians have demonstrated, early draws determine the composition of the urn. The very earliest draws will tip the urn toward some equilibrium mix of colors, and this mix will persist from then on. This is true, even though we can't determine in advance what the final composition of the urn will be. Indeed, the urn could settle into any combination of percentages of red and white balls. But the urn's early history matters far more than later history, because the early draws chart the path that subsequent developments will reinforce.[9]

By analogy, the early history of competition among racial groups can explain contemporary outcomes. In much the same way that the early draws of the urn determined the ultimate composition of the urn, those early rounds of economic, social, and political competition among the races were rigged anticompetitively by racial cartels. If the early draws favored whites, it should now come as no surprise that the urn is now mostly white.

We are ready now, in this chapter and the next, to describe racial discrimination as cartel conduct, and to understand why early history played a very important role in contemporary racial disparities.

Cartels and Collective Action

So what is a racial cartel? And how did racial cartels operate to exclude people of color during Jim Crow? A little more economic theory is helpful here. As we learned in Chapter 1, standard neoclassical economic theory teaches that market competition should eliminate racial discrimination because discriminating is more costly than hiring without regard to race. Recall also from that chapter that in the economists' version of a perfect world, the market should eliminate racial gaps. This is because people with a taste for discrimination will have to pay an extra cost for indulging such a bias, and will thereby compete less effectively than participants without this costly preference.[10] Real estate brokers, for instance, who interact only with white buyers and sellers will have to give up the additional profit they might have made by doing business across racial lines, and they will eventually be outcompeted by brokers who are willing to sell across racial lines.

But the concept of a racial cartel turns this neoclassical story on its head. Economists typically define a cartel as a group of actors who work together to extract monopoly profits by manipulating price and limiting competition.[11] For example, OPEC, the oil-producing cartel, restricts the output of oil by its members in order to raise prices for a scarce commodity.[12] Cartels can adopt many types of agreements, ranging from an informal gentleman's agreement to a formal contractual agreement covering supply, pricing, and a range of other areas.[13] Cartels can be primarily defensive, organized to gain a competitive advantage in a chronically depressed market. Or they can be more offensive and economically aggressive, operating even during boom times. Cartels can be state-sponsored, using state law to run cartel operations. Or they can be privately governed by trust and cooperation or other informal means of operation.[14]

The concept of racial cartel can help us to better understand racial discrimination and the institutional role that groups played in perpetuating discrimination. If economic theory predicts that market competition will drive out discriminating market actors, the concept of racial cartels helps to explain why markets did not successfully eliminate discrimination during Jim Crow. Cartel conduct disrupted the forces of the market, as whites engaged in cartel conduct for their own economic gain. Indeed, even Gary Becker (the economist who proposed the "competition will drive out discrimination" idea) has acknowledged that collective action by erstwhile competitors constitutes a significant challenge to his "market forces" model.[15]

First, as always, a bit of theory will be helpful. The idea of a racial cartel draws from theoretical work in a number of subjects, including economics, social psychology, and law. In early research on racial discrimination, economists acknowledged that whites engaged in a wide range of anticompetitive strategies to increase their income and social status. These strategies included employment discrimination, which gave whites better jobs; pushing people of color into particular occupations, which produced higher wages for whites; and discrimination in lending, which gave whites better interest rates than blacks.[16] But though economists described these as anticompetitive conduct, they did not focus on whites' collective action in engaging in such conduct.

By contrast, social psychologists have focused on the collective action aspect. Group conflict scholars describe how social groups form in part to gain some competitive advantage in contests over scarce resources, like social status and material wealth.[17] In particular, people form closed membership groups as a way to limit competition within the group.[18]

In a now-famous group conflict experiment by social psychologist Muzafer Sherif, researchers brought together boys in a summer camp who had been randomly assigned to different groups. After only a short while in their groups, boys strongly favored other members of their randomly assigned group and showed hostility toward boys in the other groups with whom they were competing. Sherif found that competition shaped almost everything, from the way that the boys structured their group to the nature of their conflict with other groups in camp.

Sherif also discovered a way to break this sort of competition-induced group conflict. Researchers had the boys work together on some common goal. This common task reduced conflict between the groups substantially, and also helped to reshape group norms and group structure.[19]

In helping us to see how people naturally form in-groups and out-groups in conditions of competition, group conflict theory provides great support for the cartel story. If Sherif's boys relied on randomly assigned group identity to engage out-group conflict, we can only assume that cartel conduct could make use of whites' group identity, an identity that is both easily observed and freighted with historical meaning.

Robert Cooter was the first legal scholar to suggest that we might understand discrimination as the work of collective actors. Cooter developed an economic model of discrimination based on collusion by social groups to obtain monopoly control over the market by excluding competitors. In his theoretical model, groups exerted such power through informal social means: by gossip, ostracism, and other informal social sanctions. In Cooter's view, this kind of social power permitted the dominant group to shift the cost of segregation from its perpetrators to its victims. Cooter analogized these powerful groups to cartels, even as he pointed out that such cartels were unstable because individuals had the incentive to break the cartel, for reasons we will explore. Cooter ended by analogizing antidiscrimination law to antitrust law, seeing them both as government interventions to restore competition to the marketplace.[20]

This chapter builds on and extends Cooter's ideas about discriminatory cartels. We will explore the mechanisms of Jim Crow racial cartels that kept them stable. We will look at actual cartels in action—homeowners' associations, unions, and political parties, for example—as they gain competitive advantage by driving out their competitors. And we will examine in depth the role that law played in the operation of such cartels.

The cartel story helps to explain why market forces never managed to dissolve racial exclusion during Jim Crow. But we will take up separately the question of why discrimination persisted even after Jim Crow restrictions were lifted. Before we begin that inquiry, we first need to address the question of how racial cartels remained stable.

Cheater, Cheater: The Problem of the Unstable Cartel

Despite the persistence of cartels like OPEC, modern neoclassical theorists have claimed that cartels are inherently unstable. In their view, cartels suffer from three central stability-related problems. First, to form a coherent group, cartel members have to coordinate carefully. Group members need to make sure they all agree on the rules of engagement—for example, whether the rules require members to sell products at below cost or alternatively restrict output, in order to drive out a competitor. Economic theorists call this "the coordination problem."[21]

Second, cartels face "the defection problem." Defectors are members who will breach cartel agreements, when doing so is profitable. In the case of market cartels, it pays handsomely to be the first to breach or abandon the agreement, because the first-mover defectors will earn the highest profits in a market where price has not yet begun to fall.[22]

Third, and relatedly, cartels face the "free-rider" problem. As anyone who has ever joined a group knows from experience, every member of the cartel has a reason to free-ride by making others do all the hard work while the cheater enjoys all the benefits.[23] As an institutional matter, cartels have to figure out a way to induce members to do coordinated cartel work without free-riding on other members, or abandoning the agreement altogether when the incentive to do so is high enough.

In the orthodox view, then, cartels do not play a role in the economics of discrimination because they are just too unstable to persist for very long. To get past these objections, any cartel theory of discrimination must explain how cartels can get their members to deploy the same anti-competitive strategy, to monitor each other's compliance, and to continue to cooperate even when they are tempted to defect or free-ride.

It is worth pausing here to note that reality seems to contradict neo-classical theory. Notwithstanding their supposed instability, cartels have had long and fruitful lives in a wide range of markets—from sugar, rubber, and steel to electric lamps, aluminum, chemicals, and explosives. Indeed, some market cartels like DeBeers (diamonds) and OPEC (oil) have been around for decades.[24]

How then do we account for cartel stability? Anthropologists have pointed out that among other things, punishment and reputation can play an important role in getting past the defection and free-riding problems in any joint enterprise like cartels. If some cartel members punish others for cheating, then members find it less costly to abide by the cartel rules, and more costly to sell across cartel lines. Of course, punishing that involves anything more than minimal ostracism is costly, and we run into the second-order problem of how punishment ever got off the ground at some point in human history as an altruistic norm. But whatever its evolution, punishment of cheaters and defectors has become a well-established social norm, and racial cartels appear to have made ample use of punishment to police racial cartels to make sure members abided by cartel rules.[25]

Law appears to have played an important role in racial cartel punishing. Public law, in particular, appears to have been quite useful in policing against cartel members who were tempted to defect or free-ride. To take the most obvious example, white homeowners and developers worked together to enact segregation ordinances in several cities to police the boundaries of white neighborhoods. In the early twentieth century, zoning ordinances like those in Baltimore, Winston-Salem, Atlanta, and Louisville legally restricted areas for either black or white residents or prohibited blacks from moving into blocks where a greater number of whites than blacks resided.[26]

Even earlier, in the post–Civil War South, racial cartels used law to restrict competition by white planters for black labor. White planters persuaded state legislatures to enact the Black Codes just after the Civil War, which strictly enforced contracts between planters and labor, providing little room for negotiation over labor contracts.[27]

Other statutes prevented labor recruiters from "enticing" away labor.[28] These laws limited the level of cross-racial contracting and employment so as to prevent a full integration of black workers into agricultural labor markets.

Private contracts were also very helpful in stabilizing racial cartels. Most notably, the racially restrictive covenant helped to police against white homeowners who might otherwise have "defected" to sell their homes across racial lines. During Jim Crow, white homeowners negotiated private covenants with each other to prohibit the sale of homes in white neighborhoods to blacks, Mexicans, and Asians.[29] As part of the contract to buy a house, white home buyers agreed not to sell their property in the future to nonwhite buyers.

Like cross-licensing, racially restrictive covenants tied neighbors to each other through private agreement. Such agreements were enforced not by the previous owner, but by the "third-party beneficiary" neighbors, who presumably had relied on the all-white character of the neighborhood when deciding to buy.[30] Even the threat of potential litigation from neighbors served to scare homeowners who might otherwise have sold to a willing nonwhite buyer.[31]

Most importantly, cartel members used social incentives to keep brokers in line. Group members used punishment and rewards involving approval, shame, and informal retaliation to keep people from crossing the line. For example, real estate brokers who defected faced a wide range of non-legal punishments for doing so: among others, sanction by the Chicago Real Estate Board for violating its code of conduct, loss of clients, mortgage funding, insurance vendors, property listings. More generally, brokers also faced the loss of their business good will, their reputation, and their status within the community.[32]

Internal rewards and punishments—guilt and self-esteem or feelings of aversion, among other things—also appeared to play an important role.[33] As the next chapter describes in detail, real estate brokers who refused to sell across racial lines reported feeling guilt about having betrayed their race and their code.[34] Once norms of exclusion were sufficiently internalized, group norms were self-administered, without the need for as much work on the part of organization members. In short, internal and external punishment worked to keep cartel members from crossing racial lines.

Cartel Conduct: A Historical Overview

Now that we know what to look for, we can see evidence of racial cartel operation throughout the Jim Crow era, from 1870 to the mid-1960s. Consider the example of white homeowners' associations in Chicago operating during the era of Jim Crow.[35] Homeowners' associations looked a lot like a paramilitary cartel. They divided up their turf on precisely defined geographic lines, much as market cartels do. The homeowners' association used ordinary market cartel tactics like harassment and coercion to keep potential black homebuyers from moving into white neighborhoods. Members monitored the racial identity of prospective buyers and the willingness of sellers to trade across racial lines. Group members approached prospective and actual buyers and sellers, to convince them to sell their property to the association. For more persistent buyers, members coordinated as a group to harass them, often terrorizing them physically into withdrawing an offer.

Economic coercion was a favorite tactic among associations. Homeowners worked together with real estate boards and banks to restrict the availability of loans for black buyers and sellers. Under pressure from brokers and customers, banks targeted their loans to whites and to white neighborhoods, where profits were more likely, because homes in those areas enjoyed higher property values. And of course, the association played a key role in persuading homeowners to adopt racially restrictive covenants, to prohibit members from selling across racial lines.[36]

Cartel conduct earned white cartel members a handsome profit. White homes were bigger, newer, and on larger pieces of land in neighborhoods with better public services than black homes, which tended to be smaller, older, and in dilapidated neighborhoods with deteriorating housing stock and paltry services. Beyond bigger homes and better land, association members also enjoyed monopoly access to wealthier neighbors. Owing to historical discrimination during the Jim Crow era, black neighbors possessed far less wealth than whites. Not surprisingly, then, white neighborhoods were also wealthier neighborhoods. Correspondingly, whites disproportionately enjoyed the benefits that frequently accompany wealthier neighbors—among other things, lower tax rates, higher tax revenues, and better-funded public amenities, like sanitation and security.

Perhaps most importantly, white association members enjoyed a monopoly on the higher property values that came with wealthier white neighborhoods. Owing to all these benefits—better housing stock, bigger parcels of land, access to wealthier neighbors, and better funded amenities—white properties were worth more, despite the premium that white buyers paid to be in a racially-homogenous neighborhood.[37]

Accordingly, white buyers were willing to pay higher prices to buy in a white market, because they would then be able to sell their property for more, assuming that neighborhoods remained white. And although white sellers had a stronger incentive to defect from the cartel and sell to whomever could offer the highest price, in the longer run, working to keep neighborhoods all white was in their best interest as well.[38]

Beyond homeowners' associations, we see evidence of cartel conduct during virtually every period of Jim Crow. In the early twentieth century, racial cartels were mostly informal white organizations with little state support. In the South, employers maintained segregation via a network of community norms. Outside of agriculture, employers and unions together orchestrated occupational segregation, essentially creating a dual labor market where blacks and whites did not compete with each other. Within particular industries, certain jobs were designated black jobs or white jobs. World War I challenged some of these designations, particularly as white women took jobs reserved for blacks, and black men took jobs reserved for white men. But the war only temporarily dislodged racial designations.[39]

After World War I, the role of government in cartel conduct increased dramatically. In the case of residential segregation, the federal government institutionalized the process known as redlining in support of a network of lenders, brokers, and homeowners' associations that engaged in housing discrimination. The Home Owners' Loan Corporation, which offered low-cost mortgages to whites moving to the suburbs out of the inner city, used redlined maps to determine where and to whom to provide mortgage support. The Federal Housing Administration adopted similar racial restrictions.[40]

Some of the most progressive social policies adopted by New Deal legislators functioned essentially as massive racial cartel anticompetitive supports favoring white workers. For example, white legislators from the South collaborated with members of the Roosevelt administration to exclude blacks from Social Security, by exempting agricultural workers and domestic workers.[41]

Likewise, private business organizations functioned together in ways that resembled racial cartel activity. Agricultural growers collaborated to segregate Mexican workers in company towns and housing in order to control them as a source of labor. White unions excluded blacks from organizing in crafts unions to keep them out of the crafts and unable to earn the high wages associated with the profession.[42]

After World War II, public organizations like citizens' councils and parent-teacher associations encouraged whites to coordinate their collective action to exclude nonwhite groups from key education, labor, and political markets. In the South, organizations like the Ku Klux Klan served as vehicles to coordinate violence against African Americans. To be sure, at the beginning of the 1950s white collective action showed signs of weakening on a number of fronts, as the Supreme Court and Congress worked to advance civil rights for a number of groups. But white cartel conduct in various parts of the country would remain strong even without the force of law to keep cartels stable.[43]

The next chapter takes a much closer look at the operation of two white cartels during the Jim Crow era: (1) white homeowners' associations in Chicago, and (2) white political parties in Texas.

3

Racial Cartels in Action

An In-Depth Look at Historical Racial Cartels in Housing and Politics

Sometime in late 1928, leaders of the all-white Woodlawn Property Owner's Association (WPOA) called members to an emergency meeting. WPOA was headquartered in Washington Park, which in those days was a middle-class white neighborhood in south-side Chicago. White neighbors were of varying ethnicities, mostly German and Irish immigrants. But large numbers of black families had been moving into the surrounding neighborhoods in the preceding months, and agitated members of the association wanted the organization to address what they perceived to be the imminent "invasion" of black residents.

At the meeting, association members quickly coordinated a defense against potential desegregation. Teaming up with the city's real estate board, residents planned to blanket the neighborhood, knocking on doors and mailing letters to Woodlawn homeowners to ask them to sign a special kind of agreement called a restrictive covenant. This covenant was a peculiar new kind of legal contract that obligated homeowners (and their heirs) not to sell or lease, or allow occupancy of, property to blacks. Typically, this agreement was negotiated between existing neighbors, and was a covenant that attached to the property itself, obligating anyone who bought the property to abide by the restriction.[1]

The covenant contained the following clause:

> No part of said premises shall in any manner be used or occupied directly or indirectly by any negro or negroes, provided that this restriction shall not prevent the occupation, during the period of their employment as janitors' or chauffeurs' quarters in the basement or in a barn or garage in the rear, or of servants' quarters by negro janitors, employed as such for service in and about the chauffeurs or house servants, respectively, actually employed as such for service in and about the premises by the rightful owner or occupant of said premises.[2]

Because the agreement was collective, it required a critical number of homeowners to sign before it became effective. In this case, 95 percent of "frontage" owners who owned land on the borders of the neighborhood had to sign.

Previously, Chicago's real estate board had been aggressively marketing the restrictive covenant to local organizations. Members made sales pitches to PTAs, Kiwanis clubs, churches, YMCAs, chambers of commerce, and homeowners' associations. The board now discovered a more-than-willing partner in the Woodlawn Property Owners' Association—indeed, the organization had formed in large part for the purpose of defending against desegregation. WPOA collected what members later asserted to be a sufficient number of signatures on the covenant to forestall an imminent black invasion of a white neighborhood. Washington Park homeowners breathed a sigh of relief. And for the better part of a decade, the network of covenants actually held the line, as residents refused to sell across racial lines.

But the front line was not invulnerable. In the late 1930s, a black Chicago resident named Carl Hansberry decided to test the strength of the covenant. Hansberry, who was the local NAACP secretary and father

of playwright Lorraine Hansberry, had acquired a three-story apartment building in Woodlawn. Hansberry bought the property (through a
third party) from a most unlikely source—a former white member of the
Woodlawn Property Owners' Association, who had apparently had a fall-
ing out with the group. The young family (including Lorraine) moved into
the building in May of 1937, on the day they took possession of the deed.[3]

The Hansberrys were not well received. Lorraine, whose play "A Rai-
sin in the Sun" was based on the family's experience moving into Washington Park, later recounted the events surrounding their entry:

> [Twenty-five years] ago, [my father] spent a small personal fortune, his
> considerable talents, and many years of his life fighting, in association with
> NAACP attorneys, Chicago's 'restrictive covenants' in one of this nation's
> ugliest ghettos. That fight also required our family to occupy disputed
> property in a hellishly hostile 'white neighborhood' in which literally howl-
> ing mobs surrounded our house . . . I also remember my desperate and
> courageous mother, patrolling our household all night with a loaded Ger-
> man Luger (pistol), doggedly guarding her four children, while my father
> fought the respectable part of the battle in the Washington court.[4]

Undaunted, the Hansberrys stayed on the property as the case made its
way to the US Supreme Court in 1940.

In the now-famous case of *Hansberry v. Lee* (1940), the Supreme
Court upheld on procedural grounds the Hansberrys' right to challenge the restrictive covenant, which appeared not to have gotten the
requisite number of signatures.[5] Although the Supreme Court's ruling
did not reach the actual validity of the covenants, the opinion paved the
way for a dramatic change in the neighborhood's racial composition. By
1942, black residents occupied one-third of the neighborhood. By 1950,
enforcement of the covenants had collapsed entirely and the neighborhood had become all black, owing to a mass exodus of white residents.

What motivated these covenants in the first place? Why were real
estate brokers and homeowners willing to abide by rules against selling across racial lines, despite the fact that they would have earned

significant profit in doing so? More generally, how did the white orga-nizations of Jim Crow—white unions, political parties, school districts, and associations among them—persuade their members to hold the line despite incentives to defect?

To answer these questions, this chapter examines two case studies: (1) Chicago homeowners' associations (and their partner-in-crime, the Chicago Real Estate Board), who collaborated to exclude black residents from white neighborhoods, and (2) white political parties in Texas who conspired to disfranchise black voters. Each of these case studies illu-minates racial cartels in action, and provides a window into their day-to-day operations. More generally, studying these cartels more closely helps us to understand how cartels tackled their coordination problems, defection problems and free-rider problems.

As we will see, these racial cartels shared some common features, though they were separated in time and space. Neither the political parties nor the homeowners' associations were afraid to use violence or social coercion to discipline members who were tempted to cheat or defect from the organization. Both types of cartel deployed the rhetoric of racial identity—and in particular the trope of the working-class white family—as a way of managing cartel stability.

But the cartels also differed in some very important ways. For exam-ple, as we shall see, Chicago homeowners' associations used law to their advantage, while Texas political parties had to fight law to operate effec-tively.[6] Likewise, Texas political parties had to work hard to cross the class divide and unify voters across distinct interests, while Chicago homeowners' associations worked with whites who already shared com-mon class interests. Let's take a closer look at each of these racial cartels.

The North: Excluding Blacks in Chicago Housing Markets

We can consider the homeowners' associations in Chicago to be the poster children for racial cartels. Tightly coordinated, well run, and legally armed with the restrictive covenant, the homeowners' associa-tion was a model in efficient racial exclusion.

Even before the Civil War, exclusionary sentiment in the North was already quite strong. Freed blacks had begun to compete against whites in the labor market. Indeed, some scholars have argued that whites abolished slavery in the North in the first place because slave labor undercut white wages.[7] But once they'd freed the slaves, whites then had to move quickly to undercut or cripple their potential competitors in other ways.[8]

Of course, class and ethnicity politics among whites themselves were already pretty complicated. At the turn of the century, whites who considered themselves native faced a big wave of European immigrants, all hungry for work and a better life. Between 1830 and 1860, European immigrants came by the millions to cities like Chicago—Irish, German, and Scandinavian in particular. Native whites had to absorb this influx, which they did quite reluctantly—anti-immigrant sentiment ran high, particularly against the Irish.[9]

Having only so recently secured their own unstable foothold in society, the new immigrants did not welcome black competitors emigrating from the South. Sentiment toward blacks greatly depended on where white immigrants stood in the pecking order of the labor market. White ethnic groups who enjoyed a better economic position and competed less with blacks in labor markets—for example, the Germans—exhibited less racism against blacks, at least initially.[10] In comparison, groups like the Irish, who competed more directly with blacks (and against whom blacks were often used as strikebreakers), displayed more racism, no doubt motivated by the fear of competition.[11]

A brief look at Chicago history will help us to understand the meteoric rise of homeowners' associations in the city. In 1860, relatively few blacks lived in Chicago, and those who did were evenly spread throughout the city. That year, the Chicago segregation index (which measures the even spread of whites and blacks in a city) measured a moderate 50.0.[12] Immigrant whites had settled throughout the city in small pockets, and then increasingly throughout the city more evenly.

As happened elsewhere, the end of the Civil War triggered a massive wave of immigration by freed slaves into Chicago. Drawn by the lure of industrial jobs, blacks began to migrate in the thousands, and then in the hundreds of thousands.[13] They came even faster after Southern cotton farms experienced a serious boll-weevil infestation, and Southern farmers began to replace their black labor with machinery.

World War I set the stage for open labor warfare between blacks and whites. Demand for black labor skyrocketed during the war, fueled by newly enacted immigrant labor restrictions. From 1890 to 1915, black Chicago residents grew from fifteen thousand to over fifty thousand, and subsequent waves during and after World War I were double and triple that size.[14]

Working-class whites (particularly the new immigrants) reacted with alarm to blacks' entry into white economic and social territory.[15] In their view containment was essential, and they moved quickly to cordon off black movement into the city. By 1900, whites had corralled black migrants into three main areas: the narrow finger of land called the Black Belt on the South Side, and two satellite districts, one on the West Side and the other in Englewood.[16] As blacks continued to migrate in, whites patrolled neighborhood boundaries even more strictly, to make sure that whites and blacks lived separately. By 1940, white cartels had succeeded—Chicago displayed an almost perfect segregation index of .95.[17]

The National Real Estate Board

Cartels worked hard to coordinate with each other in the campaign for residential exclusion in Chicago. Heading up the effort, the city's real estate board and its neighborhood homeowners' associations pushed hard on multiple fronts.[18] The Chicago Real Estate Board, made up of hundreds of individual real estate businesses, operated primarily as a trade organization to lobby on behalf of real estate interests locally and nationally.[19] In 1917, the board adopted a formal policy asking brokers to keep blacks out of white residential areas. A couple of years later, the board asked the city council to halt black migration into the city until officials had worked out lease or sales restrictions against blacks. Shortly thereafter, the board voted officially to expel any broker who leased or sold property in these new white neighborhoods to black residents.[20]

The same year, Chicago would see the city's worst race riots, and a number of other cities exploded in racial violence as well.

In the late 1920s, the board discovered the restrictive covenant. This legal weapon would come to dominate the war over housing exclusion for the next three decades. Brokers and lawyers had needed a legal instrument that would put monitoring and enforcement of racial restrictions in the hands of private citizens. The restrictive covenant did just that. Private residents still had to petition the courts, but they were now armed with the coercive force of a legal agreement.

The board and the homeowners' associations now hatched a plan to spread the covenant throughout the city, and board members became the face of the movement, speaking to churches, chambers of commerce, and other civic organizations to urge the covenant's adoption.

In a crucial historical moment that would pave the way for the rest of the country, the board put in place an ethics code provision that prohibited brokers from selling to buyers who threatened to disrupt the racial composition of the neighborhood.[21] The move was so effective that the National Association of Real Estate Boards (NAREB) adopted an identical provision.[22] Now brokers would have to risk their careers to sell across racial lines—state commissions were authorized by state law to revoke the state licenses of those brokers who violated this provision.[23]

In addition to the ethics code provision, NAREB also copied the Chicago board's idea of the racially restrictive covenant, and the agreement began to spread all over the country. In 1927, NAREB standardized a restrictive covenant to pass along to its nationwide membership, and encouraged its members to partner with their local homeowners' associations.[24]

Not to be outdone, the federal government got in on the act. The feds institutionalized discriminatory lending practices that had been evolving at the private level. The Federal Housing Authority, the Veteran's Administration, and the federal Home Owners' Loan Corporation all came together to codify redlining as a national practice. Now these agencies were prohibited from issuing government-backed low-cost mortgages to anyone other than white home-buyers buying in white neighborhoods.[25] In the late 1940s, the Federal Housing Administration (FHA) officially endorsed racially restrictive covenants and held on for far longer than they should have. Even when the Court struck covenants down in 1948, the FHA did not change its recommendation for another two years.[26]

The Homeowners' Association

The mastermind behind much of this institutional exclusion was the homeowners' association. This entity proved to be the key to private efforts around residential segregation. Associations were made up primarily of homeowners or apartment owners, and a disproportionate number of them were white ethnic immigrants who had only recently become first-time homeowners. Chicago associations typically claimed between fifty and two thousand members, and a large proportion of them were located—not surprisingly—at the southern edge of the Black Belt and west of the black community in Morgan Park.[27]

Homeowners' associations used every strategy at their disposal to keep black residents from buying into white neighborhoods. They pressured banks and other lenders to restrict access to credit for blacks, who had little capital of their own to work with, thanks to historic discrimination. The associations also pressured employers to refrain from hiring black workers and, more aggressively, to fire the black workers they had. Along the North Shore, for example, a white homeowners' committee requested neighborhood families unable to house domestic workers on their own premises to fire those workers.[28]

Many homeowners' associations did not hesitate to use physical violence to advance their cause: they organized their members to fire gunshots into residents' homes, burn crosses on their lawns, and physically break into and ransack their homes.[29] In 1910, a Chicago homeowners' association targeted a woman who had purchased a house on Lake Street. The group initiated their campaign to drive her out with low-level insults, harassment, and threats. Threats of violence—rocks through the window and gunshots outside the home—were next on the agenda. Finally, a group of masked intruders broke into the woman's home, threatened her family with murder, and destroyed everything in the house. The family moved out immediately thereafter.[30]

Members of homeowners' associations provided the labor to spread restrictive covenants all over the city. Making sure that an area was covered by covenants was time-consuming and expensive. Someone had to track down owners, gather signatures, compile descriptions of the properties, and file signed documents in the right office. Filers also had to pay drafting and recording fees to put restrictions in deeds, and homeowners' associations became fund-raising organizations in that regard.[31] By the end of the 1930s restrictive covenants covered close to a third of Chicago properties, and eventually over 80 percent of properties included restrictive covenants, a phenomenal figure and testament to the efforts of homeowners' associations.[32]

Of course, legal agreements are only as good as the monitoring and enforcing behind them. Once again, association members were the eyes and ears for the neighborhood. To monitor more effectively, associations structured themselves very much as local paramilitary organizations. Groups divided up their turf by neighborhood lines or blocks, and created networks to monitor buying and selling.[33]

Internal monitoring was perhaps even more important to holding the line. The Chicago Real Estate Board enlisted the associations as spies to monitor both brokers and owner compliance with exclusionary norms. The homeowners' association was the first to tell the board when a resident was planning to sell his home, or when prospective black homebuyers had approached a home owner looking to buy.[34]

The most important role of homeowners' associations was that of informal enforcer. Associations helped to draft informal agreements between realtors, builders, bankers, and individual property owners not to sell or lend to blacks.[35] The associations also provided much of the machinery of retaliatory punishment, namely community shaming and economic harassment. Punishment was usually swift and often fierce. In one amazing example of informal punishment, the *Alarm Clock*, a community newspaper sponsored by the Park Manor Improvement Association in Chicago, ran the following announcement: "Every case on which we can get facts where whites have sold to negroes [sic] WILL BE PUBLICIZED. Every white person that we know who has sold to negroes [sic] will find the truth of his action no matter where he goes."

In another section of the paper, the association advertised: "IT HAS BEEN REPORTED: Joseph Biondi of 7020 South Park sold to colored and has moved to 2007 W. 70th Street. He is an electrician for the Pennsylvania Railroad."[36] Homeowners' association members socially shamed violators like Mr. Biondi, and often organized economic boycotts of violators' businesses or professional clientele.

What kept these cartels together? Why didn't brokers sell across racial lines when they stood to gain significant profit as the neighborhood tipped? Blackballing and external sanctions were part of the answer, of course. But far more fascinating, members had also internalized ideas about racial identity that often proved as effective as any external force.

Shame and guilt were key. Rose Helper's brilliant 1969 study of the practices of Chicago real estate brokers shows us that guilt and shame played a very important role in maintaining the real estate brokers' cartel. Helper interviewed hundreds of segregation-era real estate brokers in Chicago about why they refused to sell across racial lines. Not surprisingly, brokers listed external reasons to toe the line: fear of economic retaliation, in the form of lost clients, and withheld mortgage funds, insurance, and property listings. A number of brokers feared social retaliation, including the wrath of immediate neighbors, loss of social status with colleagues, and loss of standing in the community. As one broker put it, "you become a social outcast among other real estate brokers."[37]

But beyond external pressure, internal shame and guilt did just as much to shape the views of the real estate broker community in Chicago. Many brokers believed that it was morally wrong to "hurt" white homeowners, or cause them emotional upheaval, property loss, and other harm. A significant number of respondents characterized cross-border selling as unethical, or as a betrayal of trust. Several said their conscience would not allow them to sell, and others spoke of the need to respect neighbors and other property owners.[38]

Racial identity did much of the work to generate guilt and shame for brokers. As one broker put it, "whether I'm a priest, a rabbi or a real estate man, I'm still a member of a race." Other brokers spoke of their obligations as white real estate brokers:

> No [r]ealtor objects to dealing with Negroes but we have that certain obligation to white people. The value of their property goes down. You want their faith, their good will. You have an obligation to your client, loyalty to your client. You have a moral obligation to your client not to break a block. It's an unwritten law.[39]

Not all brokers held the line, of course. Block-busting and panic-peddling offered too easy a source of money for some brokers. Knowing that the community would retaliate, these defectors set up their own separate professional networks and sources of capital to keep them in business.[40]

Brokers reported that they followed a complicated (and highly variable) set of rules about when property could be sold to blacks. Once the first defector brokers had sold a critical mass of houses in a neighborhood to black buyers, the so-called respectable brokers then followed. According to Helper's survey, brokers found it permissible according to their informal codes of conduct to sell in a neighborhood that was already tipping, and three black buyers constituted the critical threshold.[41]

Homeowners' associations and real estate brokers together formed the front lines of the battle to exclude. We should recall that this battle had some very material stakes—more wealth, higher property values, wealthier neighbors, better-funded public schools, and more well-connected social networks. Law and informal social norms around white racial identity did much of the work to hold the line against those who might defect for profit. In our next section, we will explore a cartel in which political benefit provided significant motivation to exclude.

The South: Disfranchising Black Voters
in Texas Political Markets

The story of brokers in Chicago is a story about preventing defection. The story of cartel conduct in Texas is something altogether different—a story of mutual disarmament, in which two separate groups of whites agreed to put aside their class differences and bond over their common goal to keep black voters off the rolls. At stake in this collusive deal was the most formidable political weapon of the time—the black "swing" vote. A closer look at Texas political history adds the all-important details to this story.

Historians long have argued about what spurred whites in the South to take away the right to vote for black citizens.[42] Some have claimed that conservative Democrats from the black belt came up with the idea to keep independent parties from winning with the black vote.[43] Other scholars have argued that the populists joined forces with conservatives because they both feared the power of the black swing vote. Historian V.O. Key finds it less important to figure out who initiated the move to exclude than to explain why: "The sounder generalization is that the groups on top at the moment, whatever their political orientation, feared that their opponents might recruit Negro support."[44]

Elite whites had begun the Jim Crow period with significant political power. During slavery, white planters in the South had almost completely dominated those smaller white farmers who owned no slaves. Planters had managed to boost their political power in all sorts of devious ways—putting in property requirements for voting and for running for office, passing laws that counted slaves for purposes of districting, and shrewdly gerrymandering districts to their advantage.[45]

Back in power after the end of the Civil War, Democrats faced a new and emerging split between elites and working-class farmers in the late 1800s. Small farmers were having trouble holding onto their land and keeping up their crop prices, and they blamed elite planters.[46] To organize against the elites, yeoman farmers formed the Southern Farmers' Alliance and the Populist Party, and by 1889, the working-class farmer had some form of representation in every state in the South.[47]

As the battle between these two factions escalated, each faction (likely not independently) hit on the idea of recruiting black voters. The Populist Party tried to recruit black voters in Georgia, Texas, and Arkansas, even though crossing racial lines risked losing a significant number of white votes.[48] Not to be outdone, conservative Democrats also went after the black vote, though they were quite secretive about it in the beginning because of the political risk. But outright exclusion wasn't yet on the table. Though both factions saw the potential advantage to exclusion, conservatives feared even more the force of the newly enacted Fourteenth and Fifteenth Amendments.[49]

In 1890, fear of the Constitution had faded for conservatives. Courtship of black voters gave way to disaffection, as white factions united to push black voters off the rolls. Mississippi was the first to amend its Constitution to impose poll taxes and literacy tests to keep blacks from voting. Over the next two decades, the rest of the South followed suit, including Texas, which moved to exclude black voters in earnest just after the turn of the century.[50]

In the 1896 election in Texas, the split between elite and small farmer had become ungovernable. The factions engaged in a no-holds-barred battle, using violence and intimidation to gain competitive advantage.[51] In the midst of this bruising fight, black voters recognized an opportunity to wield significant power, or at least enough power to be dangerous. Black Republicans had already provided a constant but small opposition to white elite Democrats. Now they began to throw their weight behind third-party small farmer parties like the Greenbacks-Independents, the Farmers' Alliance, and Populists.

Here was something that the factions could agree on—that the unreliable black vote posed too much of a danger to either side. Shortly after black voters began to flex their muscle, Democrats moved quickly to shut the black vote down, by pushing through legislation that required a poll tax and a secret ballot for general elections and primaries.

In 1923, Democrats unleashed their ultimate weapon: the all-white primary. The idea was a very simple one: restrict primary elections (or preprimary nominations) to white voters only.[52] By essentially guaranteeing white victory in elections, the white primary worked to quash the growing power of the black vote.[53]

Black voters and their white supporters now enlisted the power of the courts on their behalf. In *Nixon v. Herndon* (1927), the US Supreme Court ruled that the all-white primary violated the equal protection clause of Fourteenth Amendment.[54] Striking back, the Texas legislature tried again with another version of the law, and again the Supreme Court invalidated that version. Legislature and Court went back and forth for several more rounds during the 1930s.[55]

Eventually in 1935, Democrats crafted a white primary of which even the Supreme Court could approve. This version established a private preprimary caucus, in which white voters merely expressed their political support for a particular candidate. The Supreme Court upheld it on the grounds that the caucus was more private action than state action. But the Court thought better of its decision, and reversed its holding only a few years later in 1944, finding that the state had so pervasively controlled the primary process that the private primary was still unconstitutional state action.[56]

The battle now shifted to county politics. In Fort Bend County, Texas, local whites had formed two groups, categorizing the county's white voters along class lines. The larger faction, the Jaybirds, consisted of four hundred or so of the county's wealthier property owners, almost all Democrats (and all white, as required by the organization's membership rules).[57] The Jaybird party had all the accoutrements of a political party: an executive committee, a regular primary, and an arrangement for party expenses to be paid via an assessment from candidates running in the party primary.[58] Much smaller in number, the renegade Woodpeckers represented the county's yeoman farmers, and was home to a number of political officials who had been elected with black support.[59]

The two parties engaged in an all-out war against each other throughout the late 1940s. In scenes reminiscent of the Wild West, complete with gunslingers and shootouts, the Woodpeckers and Jaybirds fought violently over who would eventually control the county's political agenda.[60] As part of the battle, the Jaybirds adopted a local version of the white primary, in an effort to get around the US Supreme Court's decisions on state action. The all-white group held a separate preprimary election a few months in advance of the real Democratic primary.[61] Not surprisingly, given the Jaybirds' prominence, the Jaybird candidate almost always ran without opposition and then went on to win in both the Democratic primaries and the general election.[62] The Woodpecker candidates didn't stand a chance.

But in 1953, in *Terry v. Adams* (1953), the Supreme Court struck down the Jaybird all-white primary as unconstitutional. The Court's decision found that the Fifteenth Amendment prohibited a state from permitting any organization, public or private, to replicate the state's election process for the purpose of disfranchising blacks. The decision put an end to the use of the white primary in Texas. But it had taken a full century for the law to shut down this particular form of cartel conduct in Texas.[63]

Again, we could tell the story of Texas racial politics as a story in which whites irrationally sought to exclude blacks from voting. But as economic historians know well, the story is more usefully framed as a racial cartel story. Whites used many of the same techniques that market cartels used to shut down the competition—violence, boycotting, and social exclusion. The white primary was a particularly innovative cartel tool, at least before the Supreme Court prohibited its use.[64] Exclusion gave white Democrats like the Jaybirds the ability to consolidate political power against the black swing vote.

Of course, the white cartel risked significant defection by either of the two factions. Both sides had a huge incentive to court the black vote in order to achieve victory, though each side recognized that black voters could wield significant power by threatening to defect to the other side. Even with the incentive to defect, the cartel worked as it did precisely because it functioned as a mutual disarmament pact. In uniting under the banner of the white primary, the warring white factions in the Democratic Party agreed that "no matter how acute the divisions or how acrimonious the debates, neither faction would seek to prevail through making common cause with black voters."[65]

Understanding Exclusion as Cartel Conduct

By focusing on these economic benefits, and on the anticompetitive efforts of political parties to control political parties, we can understand Jim Crow exclusion of blacks as cartel conduct. Certainly, excluding the black vote might well also have been an irrational act motivated by racial animus. But exclusion was also, and perhaps more so, an anticompetitive move designed to reap very material benefits for whites.

Describing the homeowners' association and the Fort Bend County Jaybirds as racial cartels serves to highlight several aspects of racial exclusion that conventional theory obscures. First, a cartel story emphasizes that whites benefited from racism. White homeowners created a wholly separate segment of the housing market for themselves, a segment with higher property values, wealthier neighbors, and superior housing stock. White Democrats strengthened their political power in Texas, having put aside their class differences under the banner of white supremacy.

A cartel story also focuses on the way that whites worked together collectively to exclude, and the techniques they used to keep each other in line. Homeowners' associations and Texas political parties used a potent mix of violence, harassment, and legal coercion. Identity organized much of this collective action. Defecting homeowners, real estate brokers and political parties were punished severely for crossing racial lines. And often cartel members' own shame and guilt kept them in line without the need for external punishment.

Finally, a cartel story focuses on the effect of all this exclusion on fair competition. Thinking about a homeowners' association as a cartel highlights that the association acted to undermine fair competition for housing and for access to public schools. Whites rigged the game to their advantage, in much the same way cartels ordinarily do. As will be discussed in future chapters, we can justify government moves to dismantle the effects of such cartel behavior as a kind of antitrust intervention.

Before we get to that point, the next chapter will explore how these unfair advantages became self-reinforcing over time, even after these Jim Crow cartels ceased to operate in race-conscious ways. We will explore how white advantages in wealth, social capital, political power, institutional power, and property reproduce themselves over time even in the absence of ongoing intentional discrimination.

4

Oh Dad, Poor Dad

How Whites' Early Unfair Advantage in Wealth
Became Self-Reinforcing over Time

In 2000, two economists from the University of Washington published a paper on discrimination in jobs. The paper outlined a provocative argument—that segregating the races could reproduce inequality over time indefinitely, even if intentional discrimination were to end tomorrow.[1]

The authors set up a simple mathematical racial income gap model that looked very much like Glenn Loury's earlier model. In their model, a person's individual ability to get a job was directly connected to her community's ability to help all its residents in their job search. They proposed a simple thought experiment. Suppose there were two communities, one white and one black. Suppose also that each person in a community derived her ability to get a job from some combination of her own innate abilities and the community's helpfulness in getting its members jobs. (Let's say that neighbors provide our person her job search contacts and her neighbor-hood-financed public schooling.)

In addition, suppose that community's ability to help get jobs came from the sum of the ability of individuals in the community to get jobs. Finally, and perhaps most importantly, suppose also that the two communities were segregated from each other. Black members contributed help to the black community only, same for whites. What would happen to income levels of the groups over time?

This is in essence the scenario that the economists plugged into their model. And when they ran the model through the computer, the results were startling. Income differences between the races persisted over time, even though no one was handing out jobs or giving help on the basis of race. Under certain conditions, racial gaps even snowballed, as small differences between the communities were magnified by the dynamic relationship between individual and community.

What explained these results? The authors identified two important factors: (1) the strict racial segregation between the two communities, and (2) the relationship connecting a community's helpfulness in one genera-tion to that of the next generation. In this latter relationship, a person's ability to get a job depended in part on her community's ability to help her, by giving her job referrals or a good public education. In turn, the community's ability to help depended on the ability of its members to get jobs themselves. Framed in reproductive terms, the community was pass-ing down inequality from generation to generation. In our language, the community and individuals in the community together created a positive feedback loop.

The first factor, strict racial segregation, is what linked race and mate-rial well-being in the model. Keeping the groups separated meant that the community helpfulness could not be shared across racial lines, nor could disadvantage be diffused through a larger group. Economic disad-vantage essentially became racial disadvantage, by association. This was true even though no one was intentionally discriminating. Because fam-ilies and neighborhoods were not mixing racially, inequality in material wealth translated into racial inequality.

The second factor—the relationship between job-getting in one generation and job-getting in the next generation—linked earlier history to contemporary outcome. The more trouble a community had had getting jobs, the more trouble a community continued to have getting jobs. Conversely, the better a community was at getting jobs, the easier it was for the next generation. Income levels became self-reinforcing by way of this feedback relationship between the generations.

This chapter argues that positive feedback loops play a central role in reproducing racial disparity over time. Through positive feedback loops, inequality reproduces itself from decade to decade, automatically and in the absence of intentional discrimination. We will be looking at a number of feedback loops in this book: family wealth, in which the rich get richer; neighborhood loops, in which better neighborhoods finance the success of the next generation; social networks, in which who a person knows makes a difference not just for him but for his children; and institutional loops, in which being the first to occupy a profession helps to pave the way for later generations.

This chapter looks at family wealth feedback loops, in which white families continue to pass down the ill-gotten wealth they acquired during Jim Crow and slavery. Families of color have no such racism dividend to pass down. Before we investigate the details of the family wealth feedback loop, let's look at some theory on positive feedback loops.

Feedback Loops: Some Basic Theory

The concept of positive feedback loops has its roots in a new genre of interdisciplinary scholarship called complex systems theory. A complex system is a system made up of individual agents that dynamically interact with each other to produce interesting patterns of behavior. A sand pile is a complex system, with individual sand grains that shift over time in patterns, as in an avalanche. A stock market is a complex system made up of buyers and sellers, in which we see bubbles and crashes. Neighborhoods, body tissue, and ant colonies all are examples of complex systems, as people, cells, and ants follow simple rules that produce complex patterns.

Scholars from all manner of disciplines have recently begun to ask whether a universal set of rules governs the dynamics of these systems.[2]

Scholars say that a system is complex when it displays dynamic patterns that are visible only at the level of the collective, but not at the level of the individual agent. So, for example, at the simplest level, a single ant in a colony follows simple rules like "follow the scent trail of the ant in front of you." But at the level of the collective colony, we see coordinated patterns of behavior. Ant colonies send out foraging expeditions to locate food, and relocate to higher ground after a flood. Scientists can't predict or explain these behaviors just by looking at the conduct of the individual ant. The collective behavior emerges only at the level of the group.

Many complex systems also display particular patterned behavior called "phase transitions." In a phase transition, change occurs suddenly and dramatically, after long periods of steady or uniform behavior. After a long period of heating peacefully, water suddenly boils and then escapes into steamy vapor. After a period of building in value, the real estate market unexpectedly crashes. The racial composition of neighborhoods changes quickly once the numbers reach a certain threshold or "tipping point."[3]

Often, these phase transition patterns are created by something called a positive feedback loop. When a system's output "feeds back" to become part of the system's input, change accelerates over time, at first slowly and then very quickly. For example, gossip spreads slowly at first and then catches fire, as the number of people in a social network who have heard the rumor reaches critical mass. The dynamics of spreading gossip, like the spread of an epidemic or a wildfire or a fashion trend, are governed by feedback loops.

Economists have begun to investigate the role that these feedback loops play in market competition. Neoclassical economists have always preached that the economy is governed by negative feedback loops, or "diminishing returns," in which the effect of change is dampened as the system moves toward equilibrium. For most markets, products that lead the market eventually run into limits having to do with price and demand, and eventually the market reaches a stable equilibrium. Prices are stable, market share is stable, and all is well.

But a number of economists have challenged the law of diminishing returns. Some have suggested that in certain circumstances, markets actually display increasing returns. As early as the 1950s, economists like Gunnar Myrdal and Nicholas Kaldor were pointing out that some markets display "circular and cumulative causation," in which demand produces even more demand.[4]

More recently, economists like Brian Arthur and Paul Krugman have focused on the role of positive feedback loops in high-technology markets. Increasing returns are returns that keep growing in the same direction—that which is ahead gets further ahead, and that which is behind falls further behind. Increasing returns don't generate a nice, stable equilibrium. Instead, they generate a sort of snowballing effect, as that which gains success succeeds even more, and that which suffers loss loses even more. If a competitor in the market gets ahead, by chance or by some sort of nefarious behavior (as we will see), then increasing returns can magnify that early advantage, and the early winner can go on to lock in the market. The notion of increasing returns turns upside down many of the conventional models of how the economy works.[5]

This idea of increasing returns played a central role in the litigation against Microsoft for antitrust violations in connection with operating systems software.[6] In the 1990s, the US government filed a complaint alleging that Microsoft had anticompetitively pushed computer manufacturers to deal exclusively with the company by requiring manufacturers to pay double royalties if they loaded their computers with some operating system other than Windows. In 1995, Judge Stanley Sporkin issued a ruling agreeing with the US government, and noted that these anticompetitive strategies were layered on top of a market that already provided strong "natural" advantages to Microsoft, because the operating systems market displayed "increasing returns."[7]

As Judge Sporkin explained, increasing returns existed because of a positive feedback loop relationship that connected software authors to consumers. Consumers wanted to buy a computer with an operating system that had a very wide range of applications software available. Software authors wanted to write applications software for an operating system with a high number of consumers who would buy their products. Every increase in software authors produced an increase in consumers, and every increase in consumers triggered an increase in software authors. Success produced more success. Them that had, got even more, to paraphrase a Billie Holiday song.

What can the idea of increasing returns and anticompetitive conduct teach us about race relations? Plenty, as it turns out. The central argument of this book is that racial disparity emerges from positive feedback loops that reproduce racial difference over time. Like Microsoft, whites engaged in early anticompetitive conduct to get ahead in key markets—jobs, education, and housing, to name the most relevant. That early unfair racial advantage now reproduces itself through increasing returns, by way of positive feedback loops that are embedded in every day social structures like the family and the neighborhood.

More specifically, most of us derive our well-being from our networks. In particular, we rely on four basic types of social "network" arrangements—(1) families, (2) friends and colleagues, (3) neighborhoods, and (4) workplaces and other kinds of market-based institutions. As we will see in this chapter, each of these networks contains a positive feedback loop that translates early racial advantage to later advantage.

In family wealth feedback loops, for example, families pass wealth to other family members and to their children. Early anticompetitive conduct garnered for whites additional wealth, acquired on the backs of slaves or from victims of white cartel conduct in unions, homeowners' associations and political parties. That additional wealth has been passed down from generation to generation. More importantly, that additional wealth has permitted subsequent generations of white families to earn even more wealth. Let's examine this and other positive feedback loops in detail.

Network Feedback Loops in Action

Family Wealth Feedback Loops

When it comes to differences among the races, inherited wealth is where much of the action is. Although the gap in income between whites and blacks has closed very slightly in recent history, the racial gap in wealth among races remains staggeringly large. Whites own five times the wealth that blacks and Latinos do. The net worth of a typical black family falls between 10 to 20 percent of the net worth of a white family.[8] As of 1999, the typical black family had a net worth of $8,000, compared to $81,000 for a white family.[9] Similar figures for 2002 put the average net worth of a Latino family at $7,932.[10] And of course, the wealth gap for both groups has widened dramatically, owing to the recent economic downturn and the crash in the real estate market.[11]

Why does the racial wealth gap persist? Family wealth feedback loops are a big part of the answer. Each new generation uses the wealth from the previous generation to pass down to the next generation. White wealthy families tend to remain wealthy over time, because earlier wealth breeds more wealth in subsequent generations. Poor families of color, on the other hand, tend to remain poor, because disadvantage also reproduces itself over time.

We can trace a big fraction of this country's current wealth to the wealth passed by parents to children. By some estimates, eliminating intergenerational transfers would eventually reduce US wealth by as much as 50 percent.[12] But of course not all family wealth loops are equal. White families pass down far more than families of color, and family transfers contribute a great deal to racial wealth differences, particularly at the bottom and top of wealth brackets.[13]

Indeed, racial differences in parental wealth are a central factor in the contemporary racial wealth gap.[14] In a study on racial patterns of wealth accumulation, economists Maury Gittleman and Edward Wolff followed white and black families over time to see what factors most affected the families' accumulation of wealth. Family inheritance was at the top of the list, and inheritance included both transfers passed down to children after death and transfers made while the previous generation was still alive. Wolff and Gittleman's findings also help to explain differences in savings rates. Savings rates differed among races because income and wealth differed. Once the authors controlled for income, they found that savings rates were the same.[15]

We can actually trace the starting point for race differences in wealth even farther back, to Jim Crow and slavery. Unfortunately, consistent wealth data isn't available from those periods. But economist Kirk White uses a range of indicators and a theoretical model to conclude that the dramatic wealth differences at emancipation—when black former slave families began with zero net worth—and the impact of segregated schooling likely explains the majority of modern wealth differences. White's model demonstrates that self-reproducing wealth inequalities can link historic discrimination to contemporary outcomes.[16]

What would have happened if the government had made good on its promise of forty acres and a mule to American former slaves? Land ownership would have constituted a significant source of wealth for a group. But the little land that the Freedman's Bureau did manage to redistribute went mostly to Northern whites, and many of the few blacks who somehow got title to land saw their title fall in the face of white claim to ownership.[17]

For Latinos, many Mexicans also began their competition in the US with zero wealth. Land invasion and fraud stripped them of their primary wealth in conjunction with the formation of the American Southwest. The US government took Mexican land by force—Mexico ceded over half its territory in the Peace Treaty that followed the US-Mexican war.

Although the treaty purported to guarantee rights of title to land owned by Mexicans, communally owned lands were not recognized by the American property regime, and American courts and land speculators dispossessed a great deal of even privately owned land.[18] Such transfers, like stolen labor and the ownership of slaves, created initial wealth differences that help to explain modern wealth differences.

So how does the family wealth feedback loop work, exactly? Two important types of family transfer help to reproduce wealth differences over time. First, white parents help their children to make a down payment on a house far more often than do nonwhite parents. Second, white parents help with college tuition, which boosts a child's future earnings and wealth as well. Nonwhite parents can't afford to provide this kind of help to their children nearly as often. Let's look more closely at each kind of transfer.

Home, Sweet Home

For most people, home ownership makes up the biggest fraction of family wealth, primarily because home equity appreciates over time. According to some estimates, home equity makes up more than a third of a household's nonpension wealth.[19]

But not all households are equal when it comes to homeownership. The statistics reveal huge racial differences in rates of ownership. Whites own homes far more often than blacks or Latinos. The U.S. Census Bureau in 2011 reports that 73 percent of whites owned homes, but only 45 percent of black and 46 percent of Latino households were home-owners, and these differences are at least partly explained by the recent mortgage crisis of 2008.[20]

What else explains these racial differences in ownership? One major factor is the racial differences among people's ability to help their children with a down payment. Twenty-seven percent of whites get parental help in making a down payment to purchase a house, compared to only 7 percent of blacks.[21] According to the economists, a full 25 percent of the racial gap in home ownership can be explained by the racial differences in getting parental assistance.[22]

What's more, even for families who do get help, the amount of help varies widely among the races. Families of color who do get help get much less than whites, and frequently don't get enough help to actually make the down payment. Not surprisingly, families who can't get enough help with the down payment are less likely to apply for mortgages, even when they have sufficient income to make the monthly payments. Alternatively, they buy homes later than those who get help, and lose precious time to build equity.

Making things worse, not all homeowners have enjoyed the same rates of return. Owing to restrictive covenants, white homeowners historically were able to benefit from the higher appreciation rates associated with white neighborhoods during the era of Jim Crow. For that period of time, white homeowners enjoyed a monopoly on bigger houses on bigger and better property, and as a result accumulated even more wealth.

Widening the gap, whites alone got to take advantage of the dramatic rise in home values in the 1970s, owing to segregation. In contrast, black property in the 1970s was still located in segregated neighborhoods, with far less collective wealth and with deteriorating housing stock.[23]

Historically accumulated wealth plays a central role in modern home ownership differences. Most importantly, with the benefit of accumulated generational wealth, whites are far more able to buy into neighborhoods with well-financed public schools and relatively wealthy neighbors. And the same can be said for each successive generation. Decade after decade, whites are able to capitalize on the advantage of home ownership, and those groups that historically were excluded from white neighborhoods cannot, owing to those cumulative wealth differences.[24]

The Old College Try

White families are also far more able to help their children with college tuition. Having a college degree makes a big difference in the amount of wealth a person will accumulate over her lifetime. But as anyone who recently has priced college tuition knows, in college financing most families need to draw on existing wealth to pay for college in the first place. As college costs continue to skyrocket, families are increasingly likely to take out home equity loans or draw on other financial assets to pay for college.[25]

Racial gaps show up, not surprisingly, in parental ability to help with college tuition and corresponding college attendance. Sociologist Dalton Conley has studied racial gaps at several key points in a student's educational career. Conley's research has uncovered two important findings.

First, he found that family net worth was very strongly correlated to whether someone finished college and got an undergraduate degree. The more wealth parents had, the more likely the child was to attend college and graduate. In fact, doubling parent assets raised the probability of a child going to college by 8.3 percent, and the likelihood of graduating by 5.6 percent. Parents also influenced college attendance in other ways—attendance varied strongly with parents' education levels and the value of the parent's primary residence (for those families lucky enough to have more than one residence).

Conley also discovered a second remarkable feature about racial differences in going to college. At bottom, they were largely wealth differences. After controlling for parental wealth and other class characteristics, blacks were actually more likely than whites to continue on to college.[26] Because race is so inextricably intertwined with wealth, for reasons we have discussed, the kinds of differences that some commentators attribute to culture turn out to be based on wealth.

College matters for many reasons. The intrinsic value of education, the social networking, and, most concretely, a good job and an income down the road, all argue for the value of college. And the college attendance gap is a significant factor in growing income inequality nationally, not just among the races but also among whites themselves. Income gaps between someone with a college degree and someone with a high school degree have grown in the last three decades, and the median gap in annual earnings between degrees is now $19,500.[27]

Rich Dad, Poor Dad (and Mom)

Beyond passing down wealth in the form of money, parents also pass down another form of wealth—potential employers. In 2010, two Canadian economists, Miles Corak and Patrizio Piraino, published a study of 71,215 sons and fathers.[28] The study explored what percentage of sons had been employed in a firm for which their fathers had worked. The results were startling: 40 percent of sons worked in the same firms as their fathers had.[29] For wealthier fathers the rates were even higher; 55 percent of sons were employed by the same firm.[30] And at the highest end of the spectrum, a whopping 70 percent of sons enjoyed the same-firm benefit when their fathers were in the top percentile of earners.[31]

Some interesting details help round out the picture of parental help. Help from a father happened early on in a son's career: the majority of sons who had the same employer had worked for that employer by the age of twenty.[32] Eleven percent of the fathers were self-employed, meaning that fathers unilaterally controlled whether or not their son got a job.[33] In essence, fathers gave their sons that all-important first job.

We should not overstate the importance of such a study. The authors did not break down their results by race, and Canadian demographics differ from those in the US. But we could speculate that the same study in the US might produce similar results on the earnings dimension, and that white sons would disproportionately enjoy same-firm employers when compared to black, Latino, and Asian sons.

Mobility and Race: Movin' on Up

Critics of this account will ask, but what about Horatio Alger? Can't those who start out with little rise dramatically to the ranks of the wealthy? Won't incomes and wealth eventually converge over time now that discrimination has been eliminated?

The short answer is, not likely. Big mobility differences exist between blacks and whites at all levels of parental income. Particularly large differences occur in the wealthiest brackets. Economists document that 30 percent of white children born to the top tenth of the country's wealthiest people remain in the top 10 percent, compared to just 4 percent of black children.

At the other end of the spectrum, the poor remain poor. Ten times as many black children remain in the bottom decile as at the top. In contrast, twice as many white children remain at the top decile as remain at the bottom. Only 17 percent of white children born to the poorest 10 percent of the population stay in that bottom bracket, compared to 42 percent for black children.[34] These statistics help to explain why racial poverty persists even though average black and white incomes have converged slightly in past years.

A note of caution is in order here. We have focused on transfers during a child's lifetime, because these are more important in determining the child's wealth as an adult. But we should be careful not to overstate the impact of this form of inherited wealth. Even taking into account wealth inherited at a parent's death, family wealth flow is not enough to sustain inequality indefinitely. Over the course of human history, parents have never been able to perfectly pass down their wealth to their children, even when the next generation invests parental assets to earn returns. Eventually, then, the gap should close, at least in theory. But even the most optimistic estimates predict that significant racial gaps will be around for the foreseeable future.[35]

Finally, we should note that residential segregation in particular has played a central role in persistent wealth disparity. Restrictive covenants paved the way to residential segregation, as homeowners' associations policed against the entry of blacks and Latinos into all-white neighborhoods. Residential segregation, in turn, structured racial differences in wealth, social networks, and institutional networks of distribution.

Segregation produces persistent wealth differences. Residents of segregated neighborhoods own smaller and older properties worth much less, and accordingly are far less likely to pass down money for a college education or a housing down payment to the next generation. Segregation reinforces neighborhood network disparities. Children in segregated neighborhoods attend schools that are vastly underfunded because school funding draws from local property taxes. Residents of segregated neighborhoods connect with fewer people in their social network or neighborhood who can refer them to high-skill jobs with lucrative opportunities for advancement. In many ways, residential segregation maps the family, neighborhood, and social network differences onto geographic space.

Of course, those differences work to the advantage of residents of predominantly white neighborhoods. These residents own property worth more, enjoy social networks and neighborhood networks with connection to better employment, and attend schools that are funded at significantly higher levels than segregated neighborhoods. Here again, residential segregation plays a central role in structuring the persistent feedback loops that reproduce inequality over time, long after the laws that established residential segregation were repealed.

This chapter has made the case that race is significant because our country's early racial history structured processes of wealth accumulation and homeownership in a way that reproduced advantage for whites and disadvantage for nonwhites. The next chapter explores the self-reinforcing nature of institutional rules.

5

It's How You Play the Game

How Whites Created Institutional Rules
That Favored Them over Time

Most high school seniors competing for admission to elite colleges like Harvard experience a fair amount of anxiety during the process. They know all too well that grades and test scores are not enough to get into Harvard. In addition to great numbers, applicants must demonstrate that they are well-rounded, that they are potential leaders, and that they are willing to give back to the community. Applicants likely are not as aware, however, that Harvard's preference for the well-rounded applicant can be traced to a complicated and somewhat dubious history of racial and ethnic politics.

As is true today, Harvard admissions officers of the 1950s favored the well-rounded, athletic type, a potential captain of industry who could run a business or participate in government—in short, the "Harvard man." (Harvard did not accept women until 1972.)[1] To produce the Harvard man, Harvard's complex admissions process screened applicants through a multistep, tiered process designed to separate the wheat from the chaff.

In the first tier, officers sorted applicants using a "docket system," which classified applicants by geographical region and then sorted applicants into twelve "social types." "A," for example, signaled the All-American type—athletic strength, some extracurricular activities, but with academic credentials that were not particularly stellar. "B" represented the "boondocker," from an unsophisticated, rural background. "L" stood for lineage, someone who was a Harvard or faculty son, or an applicant with ties to the local community. Admissions committees strongly favored As and Ls, who they understood to be well-rounded young men.

As and Ls weren't always favored at Harvard. In fact, until 1920 or so, practically any young white man could attend Harvard if he could pass the subject-matter exams that Harvard administered. Indeed, the Ivy League institutions had depended on large numbers of paying customers in order to swell the organizational coffers.

But the influx of Eastern European Jews into Harvard's ranks changed the landscape dramatically. Fearing the flight of their wealthy WASP constituents, administrators like Harvard's president, Abbot Lawrence Lowell, moved to adopt admissions rules that limited the influx. Ivy League institutions began to require lengthy applications and personal essays, and to favor applicants who played certain sports or participated in certain class and ethnicity-coded activities—for example, crew or tennis. Harvard leaders made no secret of their distaste for those applicants who had excelled scholastically. They called these applicants the "quiz kids" or "greasy grinds," to reflect their idea that success had come from diligent effort rather than innate talent or "native ability."[2]

To be sure, favoring the well-rounded Harvard man was not just a pretext for excluding Jews. Author Jerome Karabel has documented that administrators who developed the admissions criteria genuinely believed that Harvard should train potential leaders and captains of industry rather than talented scholars. But as Karabel meticulously illustrates, the choice of As and Ls over greasy grinds and quiz kids developed in the context of a pervasive culture of exclusion. And because white Anglo-Saxon men were the first to occupy the nation's colleges and universities by way of coercive exclusion, we should not be surprised that the admissions criteria they adopted operated then, and still to this day, to favor white Anglo-Saxon men.[3]

The story of admissions at Harvard highlights the way in which positive feedback loops operate. In particular, the loops work via those institutional rules that distribute future opportunities and resources. Institutional rules include the rules that govern things like admissions to all schools, but especially to the elite institutions of higher education, or job selection for jobs that offer high salaries and special opportunity for advancement. And as the following discussion makes clear, the group that is first to occupy an institution gets to make up the rules of the game to structure future competition.

More specifically, this chapter will argue that as "first-movers" into many institutions—that is, the first to set up and occupy institutions—whites dictated the institutional rules for distributing access to the most prestigious and best-paying jobs, the wealthiest and safest neighborhoods, the best educations, and the most well-connected social networks. Not surprisingly, those rules have continued to disproportionately favor access for whites.

Before we explore how such institutional rules favor whites, we should first say a word about the concept of institutional rules and their connection to positive feedback. Much of this theoretical discussion will be a bit obvious, but worth laying out in some detail even so.

Institutional Rules and Discrimination

Institutional rules are the rules of the game that govern the day-to-day operation of an institution. Institutional rules can include informal rules, like the rules of etiquette or the rules of social behavior in the classroom, which are enforced mostly through social pressure and expressions of approval or disapproval. Institutional rules can also include formal, coercive rules that are enforced by penalties, like the rules that specify how you pay your taxes or how to try a criminal defendant for a felony. Sometimes institutional rules are both formal and informal at the same time—in certain places in the US, both legal and social norms prohibit smoking.[4]

To be sure, institutional rules are an essential component of any well-functioning social, economic, or political system. Having defined rules of the game reduces uncertainty about human behavior and promotes stability. Much has been written about the importance of institutions for economic growth, political stability, and a wide range of other social goods.

But institutional rules, particularly the kind in which we are interested, also create the potential for positive feedback loops. As economists have argued, institutional rules have four key qualities that make them prone to positive feedback—big startup costs, learning effects, network effects, and big switching costs.[5]

First, institutional rules that have significant start-up costs are more likely to persist for long periods of time. Start-up costs are those costs expended to get the rules going. In a high-tech market, when a firm invests up front in a new piece of technology such as a new internal e-mail system, the firm must pay big start-up costs. As a result, the firm is likely to stick with that technology over time, in order to spread out the cost of that investment and let the technology pay for itself, so to speak.

Likewise, when an organization invests a significant amount in a set of institutional rules—in a new way of screening applicants for employment, for example—then the organization is far more likely to stay with those rules to let them pay for themselves. If a fire department has decided to screen fire fighters using a written test rather than a skill-based assessment, absent government intervention, the department likely will retain the written process even if the test operates to disproportionately exclude on the basis of race, because the costs of switching to a less exclusionary test will be losing the benefit of those initial start-up costs and paying to start up another process.

Second, institutional rules will produce feedback when they exhibit learning effects. Learning effects are the benefits that come over time with using a technology or rule that is further along the learning curve, and has a well-developed body of know-how associated with the rule. With regard to the new e-mail system, for example, as time passes not only do people become more efficient at using the system, but the technology develops a storehouse of related knowledge as use moves further along the learning curve. Perhaps the e-mail system is configured appropriately so that it can be accessed via hand-held devices or from remote locations at nonorganization computers. This storehouse of related know-how and the progress on a learning curve makes the current rule even more valuable when compared to an untested alternative. Just as learning curves affect the switch to another e-mail system, so too they will affect the switch to another hiring system.

Third, institutional rules can also produce positive feedback when they generate coordination effects. Certain kinds of institutional rules serve as points of coordination that allow an organization to cooperate with others in some joint project. In our technology example, the internal e-mail system in an organization might permit the firm to coordinate with a parent office somewhere else; these coordination benefits are a type of network benefit that centers on facilitating cooperation among many actors.

Moving to another alternative institutional rule will require recoordination among many different moving parts or players, which significantly increases the costs associated with such a move. Switching e-mail systems means losing those connections and having to recoordinate. Likewise, switching institutional hiring rules might require the recoordination of several departmental units intent on finding applicants who can rotate among the departments. The key here is the switching loses the benefits that come from coordinating with a number of different actors.

Fourth, institutional rules can become quite sticky when they create a kind of self-fulfilling prophecy. The idea is a relatively simple one: people's expectations about the future determine their present. In human decision making in general, people form expectations about the future based on past experience. In most cases, the likelihood of events actually occurring in reality doesn't depend on what people expect them to be.

But in some cases they do. In certain circumstances, future expectations feed back to determine current reality in a self-fulfilling prophecy. If you expect it to happen, it does. In a high-tech market, for example, we sometimes decide whether to adopt a technology based on how many users we expect will come to use the technology. We choose Facebook over MySpace because we make our choice based on Facebook's current popularity that even more users will come to use Facebook, and that more people will adopt Facebook than MySpace.

In turn, because we buy now based on what we expect to be future use, our expectations become self-fulfilling. We expect more users to adopt Facebook, and so we all adopt Facebook, and lo and behold, Facebook becomes more popular. Our expectations have become a self-fulfilling reality because of the network benefits value of choosing the more popular technology. This self-fulfilling feedback with regard to expectations is very much connected to the other self-reinforcing qualities of both the high-tech market and institutional rules.

The same goes for future expectations with regard to race and investing in skills. Recall the arguments about statistical discrimination. If people of color expect that they won't be hired based on their race, then they rationally will choose not to invest in acquiring a college degree (for example). That choice will in turn become the reason they don't get hired, and the foundation for generalization that people of color do not value education.

Perhaps most importantly, institutional rules play an important role in shaping the mental models that people use to interpret the environment. Mental models are the internal stories that people use to make sense of their world and interpret their environment. For example, the Horatio Alger myth is a mental model that people in the US have about wealth mobility—unhappily, one that isn't true. When one generation passes its institutional rules down to the next generation, mental models often piggyback along for the ride. Those mental models filter experience and perceptions in a way that constrains people from considering significantly different ways of doing things.

So for example, if white mental models include a generalization about people of color's value for education, that mental model might constrain them from understanding how the choice not to get a college degree might be a rational response to limited opportunity. Thus, these mental models and their accompanying institutional rules can get stuck in a particular niche, unable to move toward potentially more efficient rules and mental models.[6]

So whose rules and mental models form the foundation for this process? The first to arrive, of course. In technology markets, the first firm to capture a significant share of the market frequently gets to dictate some important institutional rules. In the video recorder market, for example, the first mover in the US market, VHS, established the industry standard around which other network participants had to coordinate, while in Japan, Betamax did far better. Because VHS was the first to occupy the market, it got to dictate the rule.[7]

First-mover advantages also operate in some labor markets as well. Organizational theorist Benjamin Schneider has described a similar type of first-mover advantage in institutional hiring rules. Schneider documents the existence of something called the "founder effect," in which employees increasingly come to resemble the original founders and top managers of an organization. This "second generation looks like the first" effect can be traced, in Schneider's view, to three factors. First, those people who are attracted to a particular organization are more likely, relative to the entire population, to resemble the founders and managers. Second, the group selected by hiring criteria tends to be, as a subset of that first group, even more likely to resemble founders and managers. Third and finally, the group that remains after attrition eliminates some portion of the population is even more likely to resemble founders and managers. Over time, this "attraction-selection-attrition" cycle reproduces employees who have the same traits (like cognitive style, as well as race and gender) as the first movers.[8]

In our story, of course, our white first movers and founders had an unfair leg up. They didn't arrive at the starting line first solely by dint of their innovation or hard work. They anticompetitively elbowed their way in, and closed the door of opportunity to others, for a significant period of our country's history. What kinds of institutional rules did they adopt, and how do those rules now reproduce racial inequality?

Let's consider the example of the institutional processes that govern admission to higher education and to law schools in particular. These institutional admission rules regulate the next generation of college graduates and lawyers. Unhappily, these institutional rules have historically always worked to disparately exclude applicants of color, particularly African Americans, from higher learning in general and from the most prestigious schools in particular. This chapter argues institutional feedback loops help to explain that persistent gap.

Institutional Rules and Higher Education

First, we should say a word about the legacy admissions. Most elite institutions like Harvard and Yale have preferences for alumni children in the admission process. To no one's surprise, this advantage ends up being quite significant, in general and with regard to race as well.

In particular, Ivy League schools ordinarily admit legacy applicants at two to five times their ordinary rate. In 2003, Harvard admitted 36 percent of its legacy applicants, compared to 11 percent of the entire applicant pool.[9] Lest anyone think this is because alumni offspring are smarter than the average applicant, researchers estimate that being the child of an alumnus is the equivalent of a whopping extra 160 points on an SAT score.[10] And legacy admits are not just the province of private Ivy League schools—most public universities that are selective offer some benefit to the children of alumni. Moreover, evidence indicates that the reason most schools offer to justify legacy admissions—that the practice encourages alumni giving—is wholly false. Researchers find that alumni donations from wealthy donors are no higher in institutions with legacy preferences than in those without such preferences.[11]

A number of commentators have argued that legacy preferences provide benefits for children of alumni of color. Given the history of higher learning, however, readers should not be surprised to discover that legacy institutional rules disproportionately exclude applicants of color. At Harvard, in 2002, underrepresented minority students made up 17.8 percent of all students but only 7.6 percent of legacy admits.[12] At the University of Virginia, 1.6 percent of their early-decision legacy admits were black.[13]

But legacy admissions rules are not the only positive feedback loop. Merit rules still favor the well-rounded potential captain of industry over the applicant who excels as a scholar. Amazingly, although the personality categories have now disappeared from admissions at Harvard, the concepts of merit that prompted their creation remain very much in place. And many of the screening procedures to choose well-rounded WASP captains are still in place: interviews, preferences for athletes in sports like golf, geographic diversity with an emphasis away from the Eastern seaboard, lengthy college applications, and a preference for extracurricular activities that demonstrate leadership and character. Each of these features may well still favor our first-movers.[14]

Race and Law School Admissions

Law school admissions rules help us to understand the way in which exclusion on the basis of race operates as part of what appear to be race-neutral rules. Our first clue is the racialized history of those rules. Consider, for example, the history of the Law School Admissions Test (LSAT). Shortly after the turn of the century, law school administrators and faculty decided to generate an aptitude test to screen applicants to law school. The effort to make admissions objective was part of a broader effort to justify moving legal education from proprietary schools and apprenticeships to university-based formal programs of study.

Likewise, the aptitude test was also part of a more general move toward standardized testing. And standardized testing is an institutional practice with its own sordid past. Anthropologist Stephen Jay Gould has documented that the wider move to IQ and aptitude testing originated in racist assumptions about race and ethnicity. In particular, the so-called scientists who designed the earliest prototypes of IQ tests did so to prove that IQ correlated to skin color, that whites were more intelligent and better able to serve as officers than were southern and eastern European Jews, and that society should allocate professions according to IQ scores.[15]

Notwithstanding that problematic history, or perhaps because of it, Columbia Law School began using an aptitude test to screen law applicants around 1920. This test was designed to "avoid the human waste of allowing men without requisite capacity to embark on studies at which they were doomed to fail."[16] After a bit more experimenting with various tests, a number of law schools joined together with the College Entrance Examination Board to design an admissions test for widespread use, in large part to handle the postwar influx of law school applicants.[17]

Notably, law schools were specifically interested in an aptitude test and not a subject-matter test (though they were reluctant to publicly admit to that fact). Administrators wanted an aptitude test that tested those facets of innate intelligence that would be useful for the study of law. As a result, law professors had little input into the content of the test, by their own design. Instead, they instructed the committee that a test that had some relationship to an IQ test would be appropriate, and left it to the technicians to design that test.[18]

Even more remarkably, law schools wanted something that correlated specifically to first year grades but *not* to bar passage scores. The committee reasoned that because an applicant could take the bar multiple times, everyone would pass sooner or later, and thus the bar posed no meaningful measure of the quality for which schools wanted to screen. If the point of the tests was to screen out in advance those who would fail, first-year grades were the more appropriate measure, in the committee's eyes. Of course, law schools assumed that the technicians could draft a set of questions that would correlate to first-year grades at levels of .7 or .8. But technicians were never able (and still have not been able) to push the correlation much past .4.[19]

Jerold Auerbach and others have documented the connection between these suspect rules and the desire to exclude certain groups from law schools. In his book *Unequal Justice*, Auerbach recounts the way in which the American Bar Association and American Association of Law Schools colluded at the turn of the century to exclude Eastern European Jews and foreigners, and later to bar the door against admission for black and Latino applicants in the early twentieth century. Law schools' adoption and then increasing reliance on the LSAT (and to a lesser extent grades) was part of that move to exclude. So also was the move to put legal education in the university and to shut down private, proprietary law schools and night programs.[20]

Given the suspect history of admissions rules, we should not be surprised that such rules continue to exclude students of color. Of all high school students in 1999 with a GPA of B or better and an SAT of 1200 or above, only 6 percent were black, Latino, or Native American.[21] Similarly, recent research on race and LSAT performance by the Law School Admissions Council reveal a significant and persistent racial gap in scores. In 2008–2009, the mean score for black test takers was 142, for Hispanic test takers 146, and for Caucasian test takers 152. This gap has persisted, virtually unchanged, over the last two decades. It shows no signs of disappearing anytime soon.[22]

So why use a test that doesn't work and excludes people of color? In light of the low correlation between performance and these exclusionary test scores, why don't law schools or universities develop a better screening device to predict performance? More centrally, given the history of testing and merit criteria, why hasn't admissions in higher education been subjected to a searching reevaluation?

The short answer is that the institutional practices that favor whites over other groups have become locked in, just by way of ordinary bureaucratic processes that grow up around any business or institutional practice. Consider law school admissions, and the use of the LSAT in particular. Law schools have sunk quite a bit of cash into centralizing the admissions process around the LSAT. Most if not all law schools use the Law School Admissions Council (LSAC) to administer the standardized Law School Admissions Test. The LSAC collects student data in addition to LSAT scores, and distributes this information to participating law schools. Any school abandoning the use of the LSAT would have to pay to develop a new test and figure out how to get students to take a test that no other school accepts.

Perhaps most importantly, a school that abandons the LSAT would risk losing its reputation and it's all-important place in the *US News and World Report* rankings. Much has been written about the way that the law school rankings by a news magazine drive much of law school policy, and the way in which future tuition dollars, alumni donations, and state budgetary outlay have come to depend on a law school's ranking.[23]

Small wonder that law schools don't make many changes to the institutional rules of admission, even when data indicate that the LSAT excludes students of color, and even when data indicate that the test is a poor predictor for law school performance.

At a more abstract level, law schools retain an admissions test that disproportionately excludes students of color because they think it measures something real about the merit of applicants. In the law school "mental model" of merit, student qualifications are constructed around high performance on standardized testing or good undergraduate grades. Some have pointed out the way in which the mental model of merit that ranks people by grades or performance both reflects and rationalizes a system that disproportionately awards resources to one group. According to this argument, we justify the exclusion of people of color from law schools by arguing that white students deserve admission because they did well on the LSAT and got good grades.[24] In this way, the mental models that structure our understanding of merit are tied closely to the country's history of white privilege.

To be sure, this narrative risks an overly static view of the world, as is true of the lock-in model more generally. The world does change, as do people's mental models. Some schools briefly experimented with waiving the LSAT for undergraduates from their home institutions with certain qualifications, and an American Bar Association committee has voted twice in straw polls to remove the LSAT requirement, in part for the reasons discussed.[25] But the ideology of merit dies hard, and is likely to persist so long as whites continue to enjoy disproportionate admission.[26]

Before we close the chapter, we should say a word about power. The story of institutional feedback is a story that incorporates power explicitly into the analysis. In the case of higher education admissions, the white male founders who adopted the screening criteria did not just happen to be the first-movers. Instead, they had exercised coercive power in order to control the operation of higher education, and in so doing, monopolized control of institutional distribution rules as well.

Political scientists call this particular form of institutional feedback "increasing returns to power"—a situation in which "victors (or colonizers) at one stage impose institutional solutions that reflect and entrench their interests, thus biasing outcomes in the next round."[27] The well-known case of *Johnson v. McIntosh* (1823) illustrates the idea that rules of distribution are part of the feedback loop that reproduces unfair advantage over time.[28] In that case, the US Supreme Court upheld the US government's right to extinguish Native American land title. The case involved a dispute between a party who claimed title by way of purchase from Native Americans, and a party who claimed title by way of a federal land patent. The Supreme Court ruled that as part of the doctrine of "land discovery," governments were entitled to extinguish the land rights of the indigenous occupants of the land that colonizers "discovered."[29] Colonizers not only expropriated native lands, but also were able to impose rules of distribution that favored such expropriation.

Likewise, institutional rules about how we distribute things like housing and jobs reproduce the interests of whites who coercively excluded people of color from competition. Again, the argument is not necessarily that these rules reproduced those interests in a vulgar way, as with legacy admissions. Rather, institutional ideas about what counts as merit, like ideas about what constitutes land discovery, inevitably and unsurprisingly favor those who have coercively occupied the field.

Although merit is about what you know, the old saying goes that what really counts is whom you know. The next chapter discusses in more detail the way that social and neighborhood networks serve to reinforce racial privilege automatically, even in the absence of intentional discrimination.

6

Not What You Know, but Who You Know

How Social Networks Reproduce Early Advantage

Students who took shop classes at Glendale High in Baltimore in the 1970s and 1980s might remember Tim Spano, a white shop teacher who taught brick masonry at the public school for many years. By all accounts, Mr. Spano was one of those memorable teachers, offering guidance and mentoring even to students who hadn't taken his class.

Sometime in the late 1980s, two black students, Jermaine Decker and Allen Howard, took a shop class from Mr. Spano. Both Jermaine and Allen would later report that they found Mr. Spano to be a terrific teacher who cared deeply about his students. But both would also report that they hadn't asked for Spano's help when looking for a job.

It wasn't that Spano had no interest in them. In fact, Spano had been the one to push Jermaine to participate in a statewide trade competition. Still, Jermaine didn't contact Spano when he went looking for a work-study job his junior year. Likewise, Allen didn't put Spano's name down as a reference when applying for jobs, even though Spano had said he could. "He never really set up no jobs or nothing like that," Allen said later, "but he said if he knew somebody that needed some people, he would recommend me."

Mr. Spano did set up quite a few jobs for two of his white students, Jeff Packer and Danny O'Brien, who were in the same class as Jermaine and Allen. Spano helped Jeff get a work-study permit, and then tapped personal connections to help Jeff get his second work-study job. Spano also helped Danny to get a work-study job with one of Spano's former students and after that, five more jobs in brick laying and tile. "He'd find us jobs, whatever we wanted," reported Jeff. "He gave me a lot of side jobs."

Was Spano discriminating based on race? Sociologist Deirdre Royster, who studied the Glendale program extensively, found no evidence of that. Spano's black students routinely got jobs through formal job placement and work-study programs at Glendale. Spano regularly offered help to all his students, regardless of race. But white students, who were able to create more of a "natural" connection to Spano and other white shop teachers, got a much more valuable kind of help—an informal work-study program for white students, based on the teachers' social network out in the field.

In this informal network, Mr. Spano and two other teachers who ran the electrical construction shop went all out for their mentees. They made phone calls for students, drove them in neighborhood car pools, vouched for them to bosses and foremen, got them interviews, and even sometimes hired them on the spot for jobs on which they were working. White students also often got the benefit of the doubt when it came to a brush with the law, thanks to their mentors. No such luck for the school's black and Latino students, who on the whole ended up in jobs with lower wages and less opportunity to move up.[1]

Social Network and Social Capital

Like family networks, social networks and the capital embedded in these networks also reproduce racial inequality. Social networks distribute a great deal of value because they enable a network member to draw direct support from their closest contacts, and also indirect support from a more loosely connected group of contacts. This chapter explores how social networks can reproduce social inequality over time. In particular, we will investigate the network dynamics of job referral networks.

First, let's review some basic ideas about networks and social capital. Robert Putnam's best-selling book *Bowling Alone* has helped to revive and popularize the concept of social capital, but the idea is actually quite an old one, with its roots in classic works in sociology.[2] The earliest definition of social capital divided social capital into two parts: (1) the structural network of relationships, and (2) the resources that get distributed along those networks, in our case, the information that is connected to searching for and getting a job for a network member.[3] This division of structure and resources is a useful one for understanding the connection between networks and persistent inequality.

We can think of the structure of a network as its basic architecture or "topology." Imagine a map or diagram, of the sort that airlines use to illustrate their routes, depicting basic structural information of people and the connections among them in the aggregate—who is connected to whom, the number of links each member has to her neighbors and people her neighbor knows, and the locations of the network "hubs." A diagram can show whether the network is regular (meaning each person has the same number of connections) or random (with a varying number of links for each member). The diagram can also show whether the links are unidirectional, meaning the relationship only runs one way, or bidirectional, indicating a reciprocal, two-way relationship.

Sociologists and now economists have done much work to identify what key features of a network are most important for job referrals. One key feature is the network's size. Generally speaking, bigger is better—a network with more people in it provides more access to potential employment.[4] But a bigger network doesn't always increase a person's access to potential employment. When a larger social network contains a significant number of people who are also looking for work, competition among network members can mean that bigger networks are worse.[5]

In addition to size, a person's chance for a job referral is also affected by the density of a network's links—roughly, the number of links per node in the network. Economists have demonstrated that job referral networks might well have some critical density of links, below which a network will fall apart and leave jobseekers in a community isolated. Above the critical number of links, the network hangs together and information can get passed from member to member. Below the critical number, the network falls apart, because the network has too few connections from one node to nodes quite far away.

Imagine a hierarchical network, in which workers are ranked by how far removed they are from direct access to a job. At the top of the network are layers of people who directly know an employer and at the bottom of the hierarchical network are people who do not have access directly to the employer.

In this network, the trick is to be able to climb the ladder of referrals. To get a job, people at the bottom of the hierarchical ranking must get referrals from intermediate layers of people. The probability that a job seeker gets referred for the job will depend on how many links each jobseeker has to the next layer up in the hierarchy, and on how well linked the succeeding layers are as one moves up the hierarchy.

Networks in which the layers are densely connected make for better chances of referral and employment, particularly for those further down the referral chain. If the layers are well connected, then a jobseeker further down the chain can expect to find some pathway to employment up the hierarchy, climbing each layer through a chain of referrals. If the layers are poorly connected, then the potential "chain of referrals" pathway to a job falls apart, and the jobseekers toward the bottom become stranded.

These networks display some special features that have a big impact on job seeking. Intuitively, one might expect that the jobseeker's chances at a job will increase or diminish gradually, as the network hierarchy layers are more or less well-connected. But the research shows something quite unexpected. In fact, networks show a critical threshold in the relationship between the density of referral links and the chances of employment for network members. [6] Above this threshold level, the network provides a counterintuitively high rate of employment for jobseekers, even for those quite far down in the hierarchy. Below the threshold level, the probability of getting a job referral for someone at the bottom of the referral chain drops to zero very quickly.

Why is this so? It turns out that a relatively narrow range of connectivity makes all the difference between a network that has enough pathways for a jobseeker to connect to a job and a network that disintegrates before the jobseeker can connect to employment. Job referral networks that show this property exhibit what we call "phase transitions." In moving from water to steam, relatively small changes in temperature make a very big difference in the state of water. Likewise, in referral networks, small changes in the linking of nodes to each other and the corresponding probability of referral can mean the difference between a well-functioning network and one that creates a marginal class.

Another very important feature of network topology that affects information flow in job referral networks is the strength of the ties that members have. Sociologist Mark Granovetter has famously defined the strength or weakness of a tie as depending on the amount of time, social intensity, intimacy (mutual confiding), and reciprocal nature of the tie.[7] The strength of a tie between network members turns out to be a very important feature of network structure, particularly with regard to job referral networks.

Interestingly, scholars do not agree on whether strong ties or weak ties are more effective in general for transmitting information about jobs across a network. One school of thought argues that, at least in the case of more mature workers, strong ties increase a person's chances of connecting to people who have the authority to influence hiring decisions.[8] To ask someone in power to intervene in a hiring decision, the job candidate must have a fairly strong direct relationship to the decision maker, or must know someone else who knows the decision maker quite well.

In contrast, a competing school of thought championed by Granovetter argues that weak ties actually work better. Those people that you don't know all that well—more casual acquaintances or friends of friends—pass along new and different information, different at least from the information shared among the group you already know.[9] Because weak ties connect groups who would otherwise not know each other, weak ties may bridge disconnected segments of a network and give a candidate much more search space, both in terms of nodes to which they are not otherwise connected and the information that those contacts might have.[10]

A third school of thought focuses on something called "structural holes." Structural holes are places in the network in which a connection between two network members also bridges together two clusters of contacts that would otherwise have very little contact with each other. These holes give the gatekeepers a great deal of entrepreneurial opportunity and power because they are essential to bringing together groups that might not connect more naturally. More generally, ties across the holes give a network the ability to hang together coherently, so as to distribute resources across widely diverse actors and widely diverse resources.

So much for network structure. What about resources that the network distributes? In social networks, the value of the network depends on the type of resources that the network can make available. In terms of direct support, network contacts can supply money, childcare, mentoring, support, transportation, and an economic safety net in time of need.[11] Job referral networks work primarily to pass along information. Employers fill well over half of all jobs via personal referrals.[12] Job networks work because they transmit information about potential job openings, the quality of potential candidates, and the quality of the job.

Information flows both ways in the job referral network. Employers use network referrals because the referees will often screen in advance prospective candidates for desirable qualities.[13] On the other side, a network contact can also advise a new worker about the culture of a new place. Indeed, it turns out that gossip networks are good for business. Through gossip, members of a network can pass along valuable information about the way an organization does business.[14]

Job networks also distribute influence and power. Here, the status of the network member matters a great deal to the value of a jobseeker's connection to the member. For example, job network contacts often persuade employers by going to bat for a candidate, putting their personal reputation on the line. Likewise, network connections can push a network member to conform to company rules and toe the party line.[15] In this regard, the status of a network contact can be quite important in terms of the degree of influence she has with a prospective employer, or the power she potentially exerts over people who might provide the jobseeker with employment. To that end, a network contact's employment status, and her position in the institutional hierarchy, shape the resources that flow through the network.

Sociologists have pointed out that when it comes to network position, social networks tend to sort along a range of factors, including race and class. Thus, if whites have more highly-placed contacts with better information and more power, then their white network colleagues are more likely to benefit from such contacts, and are also more likely to find jobs that are better placed and powerful themselves, relatively speaking.[16]

Now that we know something about network structure and network resources, we can say something meaningful about network dynamics and the way in which social networks function to reproduce racial inequality, even in the absence of intentional discrimination. Recall the feedback loop that Glenn Loury described. In Loury's framework, individual outcomes—jobs, wealth, and education, for example—are a function of the structure and resources in a person's social networks. Someone who is linked to a social network of contacts who are well-employed, well-educated, and wealthy is more likely to get a good job, a good education, and earn wealth. Someone whose contacts are under-employed, undereducated, and poor is more likely to suffer the same outcomes.

In turn, the quality of the network's structure and resources depend on the individuals who make up the network. People who find good jobs become the referees for jobseekers further down the line. People who struggle to find work provide less value as a referee to jobseekers in their network. The network builds a community of value one individual at a time.

Economists have documented the way in which a person's wages and employment status are significantly correlated to the wages and employment of the people in their informal job referral networks. In technical terms, this research shows that an increase in the status (wage, employment level) of a person's job contacts produces an improvement for the person. Likewise, an increase in the size of a person's network also produces an improvement.[17] Contrary to some narratives about merit and hard work, the reality is that a person's chance of getting a good job depends quite heavily on her social network.

So how precisely do social networks reproduce racial inequality? Race shapes some important structural features of a person's job network that will help to determine the network's effectiveness. Race also shapes the kinds of resources that informal job networks pass along. Let's consider each in turn.

First, race shapes network structure by influencing the size and density of a social network. In particular, research demonstrates that compared to whites, black and Latino job seekers have networks that are smaller in size and have fewer links per person to potential employment. Social networks for ghetto residents are much smaller and the contacts that they do have are less likely to be employed or fully employed than people of color from low-poverty neighborhoods.[18]

Recall from our earlier discussion that job referral networks exhibit critical thresholds, in which a network that drops below some critical density level can fall apart, leaving some people at the bottom of the referral chain isolated and cut off from job opportunities. This highly disadvantaged group of workers is a marginalized class, which can find no chain of referrals, no pathway up the hierarchy, to lead them to employment.

It comes as no surprise to learn that as an empirical matter, owing to historical discrimination, blacks and Latinos are far more likely to reside in the layers of hierarchy at the bottom, far from direct access to employment. At the same time, black and brown networks are less likely to be well connected to people further up the referral hierarchy. Owing to the self-reinforcing dynamics of networks, people of color are more likely to remain at the bottom of the hierarchy over time, and are at greatest risk for becoming (and remaining) a marginalized class if circumstances push a referral network below its critical threshold.

What sort of circumstances might push a network past its critical point? Sociologist William Julius Wilson has argued that the relocation of jobs to suburban areas and overseas has, among other things, affected the social referral networks that link workers to job opportunities.[19] Economic dislocations like the current recession and the collapse of the real-estate market (an event that affected people of color more than most) can isolate entire communities from job opportunities if a critical number of network members lose their jobs.

Other scholars have suggested that once a group of workers falls into the bottom status, pulling them out becomes quite difficult. If workers become cut off from meaningful employment for long enough, they rationally decide to invest less in acquiring the skills necessary for getting a job. Once that happens, then the lack of skills cuts them off from employment, even if the network again becomes more densely linked in some way.[20]

In addition to the density of linkages in a network, race also appears to determine how insular network ties are. In black and Latino job networks, connections tend to be very tightly knit, owing at least in part to the legacy of slavery for black networks. To say that networks are tightly knit is to say that a person's friends are mostly people who already know each other, and those people are less likely to know other people that the job seeker doesn't herself already know.[21] Although in some ways, tightly knit networks can provide more support than looser networks, in terms of searching, insular networks are a disadvantage because they limit the amount of information flowing into the network. Accordingly, blacks and Latinos may be less successful on the job market because these groups cannot bridge the structural holes in their networks.[22]

In sum, networks can explain quite a bit about persistent racial differences in wages and other aspects of employment status. Research indicates that even the singular difference in the number of ties between black and white social networks can explain as much as 15 to 20 percent of unexplained gaps in wages.[23] Research also shows that a reasonable difference in the average number of ties between blacks and whites can explain differences in black and white income distributions.[24]

As the foregoing discussion makes clear, the key problem is that networks are segregated by race and also by class. If social networks were to be integrated, then the resources contained in those networks might be more evenly shared. Job referrals would be doled out more evenly. Family help for housing and college would be shared among nonwhite children as fairly as among white children. Intermarriage and integrated social networks, to say nothing of integrated neighborhoods, would go a long way toward redistributing wealth. So why don't these social networks become integrated?

To be sure, some part of segregated social networks might be connected to intentional and conscious discrimination. But social psychologists tell us that even in the absence of overt racism, networks remain segregated simply because like tends to attract like. Social psychologists call this attractive force "homophily."[25] As with Mr. Spano and the students at Glendale High, people tend to form more natural connections with others of their own race. In addition, people form their social networks in places—neighborhoods, schools, workplaces—that tend to be segregated for reasons already discussed. These network effects operate even in communities where there is little or no intentional discrimination. As a result, even if all intentional discrimination were to end tomorrow, social networks would continue to reproduce gaps in wages and employment status.

What about the potential benefits of such segregated networks? Some have argued that the so-called ethnic economies provide positive network benefits to particular ethnic groups. Commentators have pointed out the modest relative successes of niche economies in large urban areas—such as the Chinese in the garment trade, Italians in construction, and Dominicans in hotels—in which job referrals and entrepreneurial opportunities appear to be closely held within particular ethnic communities.[26] Some theorists suggest that ethnic economies can provide a competitive advantage because members of an ethnic network are more likely to trust each other and to work cooperatively in economic transactions.[27]

But other scholars suggest that ethnic economies provide a benefit only when the more general population is segregated.[28] In addition, that benefit ends up being smaller than the advantage that members would enjoy if they were members of the more well-resourced social networks from which they are excluded.[29] Far from being an advantage, then, niche networks are essentially a way to make the best of a bad situation, and the best will never be as good as that from which ethnic groups are excluded.

Networks represent the likelihood that people will interact with each other whether because of social acquaintanceship, workplace connection, school connection, and so on. Networks in physical space—what we will call geographic networks—have played a particular role in the history of race relationships. Resources tend to be distributed in geographic networks—think of public education in US neighborhoods, for example. Residential segregation in the US, and apartheid in South Africa, represent two institutions of exclusion that have permitted whites to monopolize resources and opportunities over time. The following chapter takes a look at the self-reinforcing nature of geographic networks in neighborhoods.

Please Won't You Be My Neighbor?

How Neighborhood Effects Reproduce Racial Segregation

In the 1990s, economist Roland Bénabou developed a sort of thought experiment to try to understand the relationship between public school financing and the wealth of a neighborhood. Imagine two neighborhoods, with the same distribution of wealth among neighbors and equal public school spending per student. Now suppose that school spending in Neighborhood A, for whatever reason, becomes just slightly higher than Neighborhood B. Maybe the community votes in favor of a bond issue for the school. Maybe an influx of wealthier neighbors comes into the neighborhood by chance. Do these small differences in spending make any difference to the wealth distribution of the neighborhoods?

Bénabou set up a computer simulation to find out. His model included some simple assumptions. First, he assumed that people would choose a place to live that was best not just for them, but also for their children. In particular, he assumed that parents chose the neighborhood that would maximize their children's "human capital"—their ability to do well at a future job or earning future wealth. Second, he assumed that a child's human capital would come from three places: her parents' human capital, from the human capital of their classmates and neighbors, and from the public school's resources. Third, he assumed that schools would be funded by local taxes, and in turn, that taxes would come from neighbors' income and property values. Finally, he assumed that rich families could (and would) pay more in rent for an increase in human capital than poor families.

Bénabou populated his neighborhoods with an identical mix of rich and poor, and all was well in the two neighborhoods so long as school spending remained equal between the two. People moved around a little, but mostly remained in place. But Bénabou wanted to find out what would happen if he pushed the level of school spending for one neighborhood just slightly higher than the other. Would that small difference change the way the neighborhoods looked?

Bénabou's results intrigued him. The small change in school funding triggered a chain reaction that involved property value, neighbors relocating, and neighborhood wealth. The small change in school finance in Neighborhood A was just enough in the model (by design) to boost property values a little. Then, a small number of the relatively wealthier families in Neighborhood B who could more afford to do so (or were willing) moved to Neighborhood A, to take advantage of the good schooling and the higher property values.

Meanwhile, in Neighborhood B, neighborhood wealth dropped as the wealthiest neighbors moved away. The neighbors left behind were not able to spend as much on public schooling, and school funding in Neighborhood B dropped.

The dip in school financing now made staying in the neighborhood a bigger risk for Neighborhood B families, triggering another round of departures by those who could afford to do so. This continued until land in Neighborhood A became too expensive for anyone in Neighborhood B to purchase. At the final equilibrium point, the neighborhoods had sorted themselves into a wealthy community and a very poor one, with well-funded and terribly-funded schools respectively in each.[1] Bénabou observed that even very small differences in school funding and school quality could potentially stratify neighborhoods by income, if the differences made a difference in property values.[2]

So much for theory. What about real life, when neighborhoods did not begin equally mixed? In Bénabou's view, given how long American neighborhoods have been sorted by race and wealth, the gulf between wealthier white neighborhoods and poorer neighborhoods of color may already have become locked in and irreversible.[3]

Bénabou also observed that once neighborhoods have sorted, neighborhood segregation is almost impossible to reverse, particularly as more time passes. Over time, the amount a policy maker would need to pay wealthy white families to lure them back into poorer neighborhoods of color becomes far greater than the amount that might have been paid to get those families to stay in the first place.[4] In addition, as urban neighborhoods know all too well, bringing rich white families into poor neighborhoods of color can trigger gentrification, as property values and prices rise higher than most people of color can afford. (We will say more about gentrification later.)

What's important to notice about this story is that class as much as race fueled the segregation. In this model, people fled the neighborhood not because they preferred neighbors of the same race but because they wanted the best public goods and the highest property values they could get, and those goods were financed by local wealth—the wealth of their neighbors.

Public schooling is one of many public services that depend on local wealth and affect the ability of residents to become wealthier. Public security is another—local wealth finances both public security services and private services as well. Thus, having wealthy neighbors means your children are more likely to be wealthy, because they will be well-educated, secure, and will benefit from neighborhood connections. Scholars call these influences that spill over from other neighbors "spillover effects" or "neighborhood effects."[5]

This chapter examines the way in which self-reinforcing neighborhood dynamics have split neighborhoods on the basis of both race and class. Because of neighborhood effects, wealthy and middle-class white neighborhoods remain separated from black and Latino neighborhoods. But neighborhood effects also help to explain another phenomenon just as important to the persistence of racial inequality: the economic differences *within* communities of color that separate the middle class from the poorest of the poor. In particular, the self-reinforcing dynamics of flight and advancing poverty explain why, in some cities like Chicago, the ghetto has collapsed to become a hyperghetto, with dramatically higher concentrations of poverty and without the supporting institutional protections that working and middle-class residents can provide.

In addition, this chapter explores another important aspect of self-reinforcing racial inequality: the role of the state. The race and class-based forces that fuel the neighborhood effects loop do not just magically appear from nowhere. As we will see, the state has a strong hand in creating them, both historically and at present. First, as always, a review of the theory will prove helpful.

Schelling's Tipping Point

As we noted earlier, the positive feedback loops that make rich neighbors even richer are referred to as neighborhood effects. Neighborhood effects are a more specific form of network effects, if one thinks of a neighborhood as a particular kind of network. Neighborhood networks (like families, workplaces, and social connections) bring people together and structure their interaction in specific patterned ways. People who in the same community join together to pay for the neighborhood public school refer each other for jobs that they know about, help out during economic crisis, and help to provide neighbors with other kinds of public goods. These patterned interactions, which emerge from the interaction of neighborhood networks, are what scholars call neighborhood effects.

We can perhaps best understand the nature of neighborhood effects by looking at another thought experiment on segregation undertaken by economist Thomas Schelling.[6] Schelling wanted to explore what would happen to the level of residential racial mixing between two groups in a population over time, given certain assumptions about people's preferences about ideal mixing rates. Schelling envisioned the city as a chessboard, where each square of the board represented a house or property parcel. He randomly placed pennies and dimes on the board squares to represent whites and blacks in their homes. A person's neighborhood consisted of their personal square plus the surrounding eight squares immediately adjacent. (Edge players had five neighbors, and corner players had only three.) Schelling allowed players who were not happy with their current neighborhood to move to the nearest vacant spot that was acceptable according to their "happiness" rules.

Schelling then experimented with a number of happiness rules. What would happen if players moderately preferred an integrated neighborhood? Schelling investigated four happiness rules in particular: (1) If a person had one neighbor, he had to be the same color; (2) if a person had two neighbors, one of them had to be his color; (3) if a person had between three and five neighbors, two had to be his color; and, finally (4) if a person had between five and eight neighbors, he required that three be his color. According to this last rule, players were quite tolerant when they had many neighbors—they were willing to accept a neighborhood with five to eight neighbors of another color.

From the rules, one might suppose that the neighborhoods would end up relatively well-integrated. But when players had stopped moving, Schelling observed a surprising result. The neighborhood had completely segregated into clusters of racially homogenous neighbors. This was true even though all players would have accepted a mixed neighborhood. What had happened?

The key to understanding the results, said Schelling, was to understand the way in which the interconnection of people's decisions caused an initially mixed neighborhood to unravel. Everyone who moved to satisfy her own requirements also affected the neighborhoods of other players. The changing racial "micro" decision making of individual agents triggered a local chain reaction, in which the moves of some neighbors spilled over to affect the moves of other neighbors. Interestingly,

Schelling had not been able to predict in advance whether the chain reaction would end quickly or continue for some time. Nor had he been able to predict the ultimate outcome based on the happiness rules he had used.

So why do our neighbors matter? Why is it important whether our neighbors are rich or poor, or the same race or different race? The short answer is that neighbors provide benefits to each other. Economists have documented the importance of good neighbors not just for residents but also for corporations. For example, moving to Silicon Valley means moving to a neighborhood with a ready supply of labor particularly skilled in high-tech, and high-tech neighbors who will create a pool of information particularly useful for a new company.[7]

Corporate neighborhoods display neighborhood effects, meaning that the more good neighbors a corporation gets, the more good neighbors are likely to move in over time. In the case of Silicon Valley, research documents that the labor supply didn't exist before companies moved in. But once Silicon Valley had acquired a critical mass of high-tech companies, they provided positive spillovers for newcomers. The early good neighbors brought with them in their wake people looking for work who were well-trained, which created a labor pool for newcomers. In essence, property value came from the neighbors.

Likewise, in residential neighborhoods, evidence exists that good neighbors can produce both positive and negative spillovers. One way that this happens is through public schooling and other public institutions that are financed via local wealth. In addition to schools, local property taxes go to finance parks, libraries, security, social support, and job referral networks, to name a few. These public goods are an important source of wealth on which neighbors can draw as they make their economic way.

We can even quantify (sort of) how much a good neighbor is worth. In a recent study of neighborhood dynamics in Chicago, sociologists Robert Sampson and Patrick Sharkey found that having a wealthy neighbor raised the income of residents more than a poor neighbor lowered their income.[8] Specifically, a neighboring family with a household income of more than $50,000 raised the neighborhood's median income on average by $7,400, while a family that earned less than $10,000 only dropped the neighborhood's income by $2,500.[9] Likewise, a neighbor who owned a home raised the neighborhood median income by $5,900; a neighbor who had a criminal record only dropped the median income by $500.[10]

We should note here that the evidence of neighborhood effects does not all line up in one direction. Indeed, when it comes to the link between neighbors and individual employment outcomes, the evidence is quite mixed. Research from two projects that have relocated the poor from segregated neighborhoods to low-poverty neighborhoods—the Moving to Opportunity and Hope VI projects—have showed mixed results. Results from those projects indicate that people moving to lower-poverty neighborhoods will not necessarily get jobs or see an improvement in their income, or at least, not during the relatively short periods of time covered by the study.[11] Scholars speculate that neighborhood effects of the sort at issue here—like the effect of attending an underfunded public school—might not be visible within the short periods after moving to a new neighborhood, but might be visible later on, and indeed might be long lasting at the level of the individual.

The Feedback Loop of Neighborhood Effects

So do neighborhood effects reproduce racial inequality? Certainly race seems to be connected to neighborhood location and poverty, and in an enduring way. Demographers have documented the fact that 70 percent of black children who grow up in the poorest, most residentially segregated neighborhoods will remain in those neighborhoods as adults, compared to 40 percent of whites in poor neighborhoods.[12] The majority of poor families of color who live in such neighborhoods stay for multiple generations, compared to only 7 percent of white families.[13]

In the opposite direction, race and class seem to be connected to the rich staying rich or getting richer. Research on the connection between affluence and children's test scores reveals that the test scores of black children and girls of both races rise when they live in affluent neighborhoods. Researchers find that having wealthy neighbors increased test scores for black children and girls of both races, but only after neighborhood affluence had reached a threshold level of concentration—the twenty-fifth percentile of affluence concentration. This critical threshold suggests that it takes a certain amount of neighbor wealth to jump start better test scores.

Equally interesting, this wealthy neighbor effect on test scores appears to drop off after the seventy-fifth percentile. Researchers suspect that in very affluent neighborhoods, racism and sexism become more of an issue, and black and female children will get fewer resources than they do in neighborhoods that are slightly less affluent. This phenomenon would explain the "sweet spot" between twenty-fifth and seventy-fifth percentile affluence. Those points represent critical thresholds on both ends—a benefit after the twenty-fifth percentile, and a disadvantage (for black children and girls, anyway) after the seventy-fifth percentile.[14]

Notwithstanding this sweet spot effect, given what people know about the link between affluent neighborhoods and good test scores and public schools, wealthier is better. More affluent neighborhoods are by definition better places to move. But like Schelling's model, neighborhood wealth displays dynamic "tipping." That is, if a neighborhood begins to slip toward poverty, or people perceive that it has begun to slip (whatever the truth of the matter might be), the residents who can afford to will move out. When residents perceive that the neighborhood is tipping—economically, racially, and in other ways—they flee.

Race is not the only thing that motivates white flight. Class might be an even bigger factor. Recent sophisticated research highlights how much the wealth of one's neighbors motivates people's decision to move. Using census data, researchers looked at the effect of foreign-born immigrants on housing prices in various areas around the city. Researchers observed two patterns of note: in mostly white neighborhoods, as foreign immigrants move in, whites moved out, and housing prices grew much more slowly than for neighborhoods that already contained high numbers of immigrants.

One might suspect that the foreignness of the immigrants was what motivated whites to move. But when researchers controlled for foreign origin or ethnicity of the newcomers to look just at socioeconomic factors, the effect remained. Indeed, whites appeared to be most sensitive to the education levels of the incoming immigrant population, and not to their foreignness.[15]

White, Black, and Brown Flight in US History

White flight to the suburbs has a long history in the US, as scholars have extensively documented. Beginning in the 1940s, Federal Housing Administration (FHA) and Veterans Affairs (VA) loan programs subsidized middle-class white mass exodus out of US cities and into the suburbs.[16] Redlining was common. The FHA and the Home Owners' Loan Corporation graded geographic areas based on racial composition as one of several features affecting the desirability of the areas. As a result, subsidized low-cost loans were available for white families wanting to exit the cities as blacks and other immigrants moved in, but not for black families or for black neighborhoods.[17]

As whites fled to the cities for the suburbs, work followed them. At some key point, the suburb was no longer the place one left behind on the way to work. It became the place to which people commuted *for* work. In Los Angeles, at some apocryphal moment in the 1990s, the river of morning commute traffic from the west side into the urban center along Interstate 10 reversed direction, to flow from east to west, as the center of gravity for employment had relocated to the west side.[18]

Less well-known is the more recent story of black and brown flight from the city.[19] Coinciding with legal changes, middle-class blacks and Latinos were able to move into the suburbs, and their departure left the urban core's poorest residents even poorer than before. But black and brown flight did not produce the same kind of wealth gains for them that whites experienced after moving.[20] More importantly, their exodus triggered the creation of what sociologist Loïc Wacquant calls the hyperghetto in cities like Detroit, Chicago, Cleveland, Washington, Baltimore, and

Philadelphia. As the people who could afford to move left the inner city, they left behind the poorest of the poor who could not afford to move, now living in neighborhoods of even more concentrated poverty. The urban center then descended further into joblessness, poverty, and crime.[21]

Take for instance the famous Chicago neighborhood, Bronzeville, which had housed many of Chicago's poor black residents in the 1950s. In the Bronzeville of the 1950s, residents were poor, but a significant number of residents were stably employed. Local businesses and institutions flourished. Cinemas, taverns, hotels, restaurants, and other small businesses were located on one of the city's most vibrant commercial strips. Organizational infrastructure allowed the neighborhood to function.

But the Bronzeville of today is a bombed out, decaying warzone, a depopulated neighborhood in which crime rates are sky-high, jobs are nonexistent, and institutions like banks, churches, social clubs, and barbershops have disappeared almost completely. White flight was not the culprit—white flight was never as much an issue for Bronzeville, given that for a long portion of the area's history, it had been segregated for blacks.

So what happened then? Scholars have traced the emergence of the Bronzeville hyperghetto to three causes: (1) the flight of the relatively wealthier black families who had held jobs; (2) the disappearance of work for the residents left behind; and (3) the city's decision to locate its public housing in the neighborhood.[22] Up until the late 1960s, black residents of all classes were mostly confined to Bronzeville. Even those blacks who could afford to flee ran up against the high wall of racial exclusion and residential segregation. But the Fair Housing Act of 1968 weakened those barriers, and opened the door for middle-class exit from Bronzeville. Those who could afford to do so now moved to better neighborhoods, often middle-class black neighborhoods, and sometimes working-class white neighborhoods.[23]

Middle-class blacks had plenty of reasons to move, most of them economic. For one thing, jobs had shifted to the suburbs (and now more recently overseas). Government spending cuts also made the city a less attractive place. Thus, middle-class families had every incentive to relocate to find better-financed public schools, lower taxes, and higher property values.

But the departure of this group—the richest of the poor—affected more than just middle-class well-being. Their exit triggered a chain reaction that emptied out the city center, in exactly the way that Bénabou's model described. The first round of departure included the wealthiest of the poor—those whose resources enabled them to move, and whose benefit from leaving would by their accounting offset the cost of moving. Their departure left the group behind poorer without their presence—without their taxes, without their social network connections, without their political participation. In turn, a new group of the richest of the poor was compelled to leave, given that the community had become poorer. Each round of departures left the group poorer and triggered a new round of departures, until the richest of the poor were still too poor to move or would not have gained from the move.[24]

In a key moment in this dynamic process, as Wacquant describes it, Bronzeville lost its key social institutions. In addition to centers of employment, banks, libraries, barbershops, and community centers closed. At this point, anyone who could scrape together the money to leave did so. And at the end of this chain reaction of departures, Bronzeville had imploded. In its place was a hyperghetto with few residents, no centers of work or social institutions, no public services, high crime rates, and little hope of recovery.

The Role of the State

So what role does the state play in all of this? Don't we rely on law to help regulate social policy so that hyperghettos don't form? In fact, a closer look reveals that law actually helped to create the hyperghetto. Law actually constitutes what we think of as neighborhoods. Law defines neighborhood jurisdictions and how public goods are financed. Law regulates urban development. Law determines who is allowed into a neighborhood and who is kept out. And in the case of Bronzeville and other hyperghettoes, law facilitated the exit of the middle class and the concentration of poverty for those left behind. Let's examine the role that law played a bit more closely.

First, law has governed the way in which neighborhood wealth is shared. In particular, the state has created the boundaries that divide the population into particular tax bases or jurisdictions—those are not natural but instead were legal creations.[25] In addition, zoning laws also have sorted urban and suburban neighborhoods into wealthy, middle-class, and poor. Zoning requirements having to do with lot size, setback provisions (how far back must the house sit from the curb), and other requirements that drive up the cost of residential housing often function to exclude on the basis of race as well as class. Zoning in the suburbs that excluded multifamily housing and restricted development to more expensive single-family homes meant that price functioned as the gateway out of the ghetto.

More importantly, state law has dictated the financing of public goods for those left behind. Most states and municipalities have continued to finance public services like schooling on the basis of local wealth, even as the middle and working class have exited the urban center. The same practice in the suburbs meant that those who were able to move enjoyed the benefits of concentrated wealth in funding their public services. Even when states have adopted some form of centralized funding in order to decouple financing from local wealth, school districts are more likely to shift to some kind of bond-financed school funding, and local wealth again becomes an issue.[26]

Second, the state and local government's urban planning decisions, particularly with regard to where to locate public housing, have also affected the racial and class dynamics of the city. In Chicago, city officials located its public housing in tall high-rise buildings in the city's historic ghetto, squarely within or immediately adjacent to the traditional Black Belt in the South or West sides. Simultaneously, the city moved poor black residents out of blighted neighborhoods so that the property could be redeveloped for middle-class whites. Many of the displaced residents ended up in public housing concentrated in a very small area in the historic ghetto. In effect, authorities had created a second ghetto layered on top of the first ghetto. Indeed, this decision to locate public housing in the ghetto in Chicago packed the poorest of the poor into in an area that already contained a vastly disproportionate share of the city's poor people of color.

To make matters worse, both the federal government and the city then withdrew social support for residents. Outlays for Aid for Dependent Children grew smaller and city officials rolled back municipal services in the ghetto, closing libraries and schools as the population dwindled. The Clinton-era welfare reform legislation further cut back on social support for the city's poor, and the focus on pushing recipients to work provided little help for residents in the urban core, from which jobs had fled years earlier.[27] No small wonder that the city's ghetto neighborhoods began to deteriorate in a downward spiral to produce a hyperghetto.

Third and finally, the state's policies on incarceration, and on the mass incarceration of black men from the imploding ghetto, have had incredibly important consequences for residents who remained behind. Over the last four decades, the prison population has dramatically flipped from a majority white population to a skyrocketing population that is predominantly black and brown—from 70 percent white to 70 percent black and Latino.[28]

Scholars have linked the browning of the prison population to the funding of crime control via the war on drugs. As part of that war, the Reagan administration pushed to increase criminal sentences associated with crack cocaine, and subsequent presidents enacted legislation to increase sentences associated with third offenses (the so-called "three strikes" legislation). Mandatory sentences and minimum rehabilitation work to the disproportionate disadvantage of those who repeatedly enter the criminal justice system. But despite the deep connection between race and prison or jail time, courts have refused to hear legal challenges to incarceration that highlight the disparate impact of criminal policy on people of color.[29]

Sociologist Loïc Wacquant has described the link between the operation of law in the criminal justice system and the hyperghetto. First, for political reasons, the state has dramatically increased admissions to prisons and jails (particularly the latter), even as crime rates have plummeted in the country's largest cities. Sentences are higher. More crimes are punished with jail time. Both of these phenomena are particularly true with regard to the government's war on drugs. Second, state policies have increasingly regulated black and brown people through parole and probation, and people who violate the conditions of their parole or probation are being returned to prison at skyrocketing rates, and for longer periods. Third, states have poured money into prisons and jails for constructing new facilities and hiring new personnel, even as the states have simultaneously cut back on social support and welfare expenditures. Fourth and finally, the state has, in a bipartisan manner, abandoned the idea of rehabilitation in favor of retribution. The effect of this shift in state policy—from social support to punishment, from rehabilitation to retribution, from infrastructure to incarceration—has serious consequences for communities of color.

More specifically, the huge numbers of black and brown men cycling through the prison system have created a serious burden on a few select neighborhoods. These are the ghetto neighborhoods from which many people exit and to which many people return after they have served their time. In 2001, for example, 34 percent of all Chicago reentering prisoners returned to 8 percent of the city's neighborhoods. Not surprisingly, these neighborhoods have above-average rates of poverty and unemployment.[30]

These neighborhoods also have much less political power to determine their fate than do white wealthy neighborhoods. Felon disfranchisement laws, which exist in several key states, disable those who are most invested in and know the most about the state's penal system from voting for legal change.[31] In sum, the law plays a central role in the imploding ghetto and the downward spiral of neighborhood deterioration.

Federal law has also played a role in creating the hyperghetto, by limiting the reach of law's potential to eliminate racial disparity. The famous Supreme Court cases of *Milliken v. Bradley* (1974) and *Missouri v. Jenkins* (1995) limited the reach of court-ordered busing to halt the effects of white flight. In *Milliken*, the US Supreme Court decided that court-ordered busing as a desegregation remedy could not cross local district boundaries, creating in effect a busing-free zone into which whites could move if they could afford to.[32] Likewise, in *Jenkins*, the Court found that the legislative remedy for school segregation connected to Kansas City could not extend to the suburbs, which themselves had become segregated due to white flight.[33] Here, the law in essence declared white suburbs to be free of the kind of legal regulation that might have demanded integration.

In sum, law is at the heart of neighborhood effects. More generally, law plays a central role in all of the disparity-reinforcing feedback loops we have been discussing. Law controls the structure of neighborhood inter-action, family wealth distribution, and the distribution of jobs. State tax and estate law governs the passing of white wealth from parent to child, via property and estate laws that classify gifts of college tuition and money for the down payment of a house differently from those gifts passed from parent to child after death. Local government law dictates that wealthy white communities like Beverly Hills need not share their wealth with the communities from which many of the workers in the informal economy (domestic work, landscaping work, sanitation work) come.

Electoral districting law determines who gets to be part of the in-group when it comes to political representation. Criminal law determines that one in nine black men and one in fourteen Latino men will spend time in prison, and that those men do not get to continue partici-pating politically in their community after they have served their time. Employment law determines whether employers can fill jobs via word of mouth or informal network referral, versus other recruiting and hiring practices that require the employer to cast a net wider than the infor-mal network created by current employees. In future chapters, we will discuss how the state might play a central role in dismantling feedback loops, even as it plays a role in their creation.

8

Locked In

How White Advantage May Now Have
Become Hard-Wired into the System

In 2006, sociologists Robert Sampson and Jeffrey Morenoff published a remarkable study on race and poverty in Chicago.[1] The authors tracked the rise and fall of poverty rates and racial make-up of Chicago neighborhoods for a two-decade period, between 1970 and 1990. Cities are vibrant, dynamic places and people move in and out of neighborhoods on a regular basis. Sampson and Morenoff expected to find that neighborhoods changed their character, if not a lot then at least a little, over the period of twenty years. But the authors were surprised to discover just how little the neighborhoods had changed when it came to their place in the lineup.

Relative positions with regard to poverty remained pretty stable. Those neighborhoods that were poor in 1970 were almost all poor twenty years later.[2] Even as neighborhoods got much poorer, their relative position in the pecking order stayed the same—that is, the poorest neighborhoods in 1970 were also the poorest in 1990, only much more so. Over time, neighborhood positions remained remarkably stable despite a high turnover of families and individuals.[3]

Not surprisingly, the racial makeup of neighborhoods also stayed fairly stable, as race was linked closely to poverty. The poorest neighborhoods were also the blackest neighborhoods. For the beginning and end of the period, poverty was highest in the neighborhoods that formed the core of the city's historic black belt: Grand Boulevard, Oakland, Woodlawn, and Englewood to the south, and Garfield Park and North Lawndale along the city's western corridor.

Indeed, race seemed to constitute the magic key that determined whether neighborhoods would remain poor. Persistent racial poverty appeared to kick in at a specific threshold: neighborhoods that were at least 40 percent black in 1970 remained black and poor or became blacker and poorer over the next twenty years.[4] And poverty wasn't just associated with a neighborhood's African American composition. Chicago had become more heavily Latino during the twenty years under study. Sure enough, the study's results showed that over time, the presence of Latinos in a neighborhood came to be linked to higher poverty rates.

White neighborhoods were affected by race as well. Neighborhoods with the fewest homeowners and those closest to the black belt experienced the biggest increases in poverty. For both black and white neighborhoods, the study showed what long-time Chicago residents had already known—over time the white rich got richer, or at the very least stayed richer, and the black poor got (or stayed) poorer. Whites who got poorer were the ones who lived closest to black neighborhoods. Sampson and Morenoff's findings suggest that race was closely correlated to the economic status of the neighborhoods.

How is it that neighborhoods remain racially segregated and desperately poor generation after generation? This chapter suggests that white self-reinforcing advantage may now be "locked in" because it costs too much to switch to a more inclusive path. People of color would have to come up with the money to buy into wealthier neighborhoods. White local governments and law schools would have to dismantle long-standing bureaucratic processes. We would have to restructure the way we distribute resources and opportunities, maybe do away with family inheritance or the way we form our social groups, none of which is all that likely. In the following discussion, we examine the mechanisms that create lock-in and its effects.

Durable Inequality: Some Theoretical Principles

In many ways, lock-in is a pretty familiar concept. Many everyday processes show signs of lock-in. On a college campus, for example, student traffic cuts a pathway across a grassy quad, because the grooves are self-reinforcing. Each time a student uses the pathway to cross the quad, the next student who comes along is more likely to follow the grooves rather than creating a slightly different pathway. At some key period, the likelihood that a student will use a different path drops dramatically, perhaps when the pathway first becomes visible as a path. The cross-quad path has become locked in.

It isn't that students couldn't take a different path. In fact, they could forge their own way across the grass, and many do. But these noncon-formists will pay some cost to do so—perhaps the grass will be wet, or too thick to cross as easily, or they will miss the opportunity to say hello to students crossing in the other direction. To put it in more formal terms, when the costs of switching to another path are too high, lock-in will literally keep students on the straight and narrow.

We can borrow liberally from economics and complex systems theory to come up with a theoretical definition of lock-in. Economists define lock-in as the point at which a market settles down into a particular configuration or market equilibrium and becomes relatively more inflexible as time passes. In the absence of some external force or shock that shakes things up a bit, a locked-in system will remain fairly fixed.[5]

The evolutionary history of typewriter keyboards competition illustrates this transition point. Scholars have traced the success of the Sholes QWERTY typewriter keyboard—the standard alphabetic keyboard found on all electronic devices today—to two seemingly minor historical events. Initially, in the late 1800s, a number of typing schools decided to use the QWERTY keyboard to develop a typing course. A short time later, a typist using this QWERTY keyboard scored a decisive victory in a typing contest in 1888. These minor events gave the QWERTY keyboard a small but important competitive lead early on in the keyboard market.[6]

That advantage then became self-reinforcing, owing to the relationship between typist preferences and employers labor needs. New typists were eager to train on the most popular keyboard adopted by the widest range of employers. In turn, employers wanted to buy the keyboard that would give them access to the greatest pool of trained typists. Each bump in the number of QWERTY typists triggered an increase in the number of employers who bought the keyboard. In turn, the keyboard's greater popularity with employers persuaded even more typists to train on the keyboard, and so on and so forth. Eventually, the QWERTY keyboard captured the market.[7]

At some point during the market competition, QWERTY's initial advantage became virtually impossible to dislodge. Once QWERTY had become sufficiently popular, typists and employers were no longer willing to pay the costs to switch to an alternative keyboard. For one thing, typists on an alternate keyboard would have to duplicate their costs to train on using the board, rendering the cost to train on QWERTY wasted. Typists using another keyboard would also reduce their number of potential employment opportunities. For their part, employers using another keyboard would risk having too small a pool of trained typists from which to draw. At some point, owing to these switching costs, the likelihood that either employers or typists would switch dropped quite dramatically.[8]

The Polya Urn

We can explore a slightly more sophisticated description of lock-in by examining the Polya urn model that we discussed in the first chapter. Recall that in a Polya urn model experiment, researchers fill an urn with two balls, one red and one white. The experimenters then begin a series of draws, in which they draw a ball and replace it together with another of the same color. The experimenter continues draws and replacements for an infinite number of times.

Now for a little statistics. Suppose that the urn contains half red balls and half white. In a Polya process, the probability that each ball is drawn will depend on the proportion of existing balls in the urn of that color.[9] At the very outset, then, the probability of drawing a red ball is fifty-fifty.

But as the experimenters continue to draw from the urn, something very interesting happens. The proportion of the balls in the urn quickly begins to "tip" over a short period of time, predominantly toward one color or the other. By chance, a few more red balls or a few more white are chosen, and these draws affect subsequent draws in a dramatic way. As if by magic, the urn suddenly and dramatically settles down to some fixed and quite durable proportion of red and white balls—let's say, for example, 60 percent red and 40 percent white. Remarkably, no matter how many more draws the experimenter completes, the proportion of red balls and white balls remains the same at 60/40.

Even more interesting, this ending proportion will vary from experiment to experiment. In one run, the urn might settle into a proportion of 22 percent red and 68 percent white. On a subsequent run, the proportion might instead end up at 78 percent red.[10] The early draws seem to influence what end point the process reaches. But no matter what the ending proportion is, the urn tips and then settles into an unchanging proportion at right around the same point in time, at roughly the same number of draws, fairly early on. This is the key transformative point that creates lock-in.

In analyzing what happens in the urn, experts have noticed that for certain kinds of urn experiments, two phases emerge. In the first early phase, the draws at the beginning of the process set the foundation for the ending proportion. Early history matters. If early in the draws the experimenter happens by chance to draw red balls several times in a row, the likelihood that the urn tips to more red than white goes up dramatically. But that same number of red balls in a row might make very little difference a few draws later in the process, once the urn has tipped to majority white.

In the second phase, the urn has settled at some fixed proportion of balls, where fluctuations have very little effect. In this phase, the ordinary forces of chance that affect the selection of balls drive the filling of the urn.[11] So if the urn contains 40 percent red balls, the likelihood that the experimenter will draw a red ball and add another is roughly 40 percent, and a few chance repeated red ball draws will not appreciably change that proportion.

Scientists call this early-history-matters phenomenon "path dependence," because the early history of the urn determines the urn's final outcome. During this second phase, we say that the urn proportions have become locked in. The likelihood of drawing a sufficient number of red or white balls to change or switch the urn proportions have dropped so low as to become negligible. The urn's early history determines its final composition.

Switching Costs

The Polya urn is a quite formal way of describing lock-in. To simplify things a bit, we can focus for a moment on the central feature of lock-in: high switching costs. In our quad pathway example, the likelihood that people will use a different path across the quad at some key point becomes dramatically lower. Why? Because the cost to switch to a new path other than the well-worn groove would be too high. Maybe taking a different path would require additional effort to navigate thick grass, or take the traveler longer to get to a destination, or require her to travel an unknown route.

In the technology markets, switching costs are defined as the costs that consumers would have to pay to switch from one technology to another.[12] The consumer contemplating a switch from VHS videotapes to Betamax, for example, would have had a terrible time trying to find Betamax videos in a store full of VHS. In the QWERTY story, typists wanting to use another keyboard would have had learn a whole new keyboard. These switching costs lock-in a particular technology because they significantly lower the probability that the consumer (or the quad-crosser in the earlier example) will make the switch.

Switching costs can be a product of the way an institution does business. So in politics, for example, switching a policy with short-term benefits for one that has long-term benefits is less likely than it might otherwise be. This is because a politician's time scale is oriented toward the short term. David Stockman, budget director for Reagan, famously refused to spend political capital to address Social Security's longer-term problems. As Stockman put it, Social Security would be "some other guy's problem in 2010."[13] In politics, short-term switching costs often rule the day even when they would be offset by benefits that take a bit longer to mature.

Racial Inequality and Lock-In

So what are the forces that generate lock-in when it comes to racial inequality? As a general matter, we can identify four types of switching costs that keep racial disparity locked in place: economic, structural, social, and political costs. Let's consider each type of cost in turn, drawing on some of our earlier discussion of various feedback loops.

The first type of switching cost, the economic switching cost, plays a central role in locking in residential segregation. As the Bénabou model illustrated, people looking to switch from the poorer neighborhood to the wealthier one face significant economic switching costs. Housing is more expensive in neighborhoods with better-financed public schools, and residents who attend poorly-funded public schools will be much less likely to be able to pay higher prices.[14] To break out of this feedback loop, someone would have to finance those home purchases or rentals.

Minorities themselves aren't likely to foot that bill. Owing to discrimination, people of color comparatively have less wealth with which to finance the switch, because they have accumulated less wealth along the way.[15] Recall also that for communities of color, parents are less able to provide help in making a down payment to buy a house. And selling their homes in relatively segregated communities will not raise nearly as much money to permit them to move.[16]

Nonwhites aren't the only ones who would have to pay economic switching costs. Whites who move into neighborhoods of color would also have to pay a price to move into poorer, nonwhite communities. Coming from relatively wealthier neighborhoods, whites who migrate across the color line to segregated neighborhoods will lose access to well-funded schools, better job networks, and wealthier neighbors. In addition, if they move into a neighborhood that is tipping even further toward nonwhite residents, they risk property depreciation, as the neighborhood becomes progressively poorer and more nonwhite.[17]

We should note here that for some white renters and homebuyers, those switching costs are relatively lower. The so-called cultural creatives—artists, young professionals, empty nesters, and couples (gay and straight) who do not plan to have children—pay lower costs because they are less tied to public schools and network contacts for children. But for white families with children, buying into a relatively lower-income, integrated, or nonwhite neighborhood can mean sacrificing in terms of school quality and neighborhood connections.[18]

But even when whites are willing to pay switching costs in order to take advantage of lower prices, the same neighborhood dynamics that produce stratification can often generate restratification, in the form of gentrification. As white cultural creatives move in, for example, property values rise to reflect the influx of wealthier neighbors, who can often better afford to improve property that they own or rent. Existing residents are then priced out of the rental and purchase markets (and neighborhoods of color often contain a higher proportion of renters than owners).[19] Owing to the arrow of time, dismantling neighborhood lock-in may require far more in the way of economic switching costs to keep neighborhoods integrated than if they had been integrated from the beginning.

We can illustrate a second type of switching cost via the example of law school admissions. "Structural switching costs" are associated with

changing bureaucratic structures. Often, institutional bureaucracy generates a network of standardized processes that evolve to fit together in com-
patible ways. Changing one process can create structural incompatibility
in other parts of the network. In those instances, switching would require
the institution to change all aspects of the network at the same time.

Such switching costs stand in the way of more racial inclusiveness
in law school admissions. Most commentators in favor of more inclusive law school admissions argue that schools should abandon the Law
School Admissions Test, which disproportionately excludes students of
color.[20] Despite the fact that the LSAT is a pretty lousy predictor of first
year grades, almost all law schools use the test for admissions decision.[21]

Unhappily, the LSAT is linked to a network of bureaucratic and
organizational practices that have grown up around law schools' use
of the LSAT. For example, law schools created the Law School Admissions Council (LSAC) to supervise the drafting and administration of
the LSAT, to collect and distribute LSAT scores to all law schools, and
to give all law schools direct computer access to applicant information.
Law school rankings (and in turn alumni donations and law firm interest in hiring graduates) are also structurally tied to the use of the test.
A full 12.5 percent of *US News and World Report* rankings comes from
LSAT performance.[22]

Assume for a moment that a law school decided to switch to a new
admissions test because the LSAT disproportionately excludes black and
Latino applicants. Our hypothetical school would have to pay significant
structural switching costs. First, the school would lose use of the LSAC
administrative network to collect and distribute information. Moreover,
the school would have to pay to construct, validate, monitor, and administer any replacement test.[23]

Most dauntingly, the school would risk its standing in the *US News*
law school rankings. Students would be less likely to take more than one
test as part of the application process, which would reduce the school's
applicant pool significantly (and affect the school's selectivity scores,
which are based on the number of acceptances divided by the number
of applicants). The news magazine would have to recalibrate its rankings

to reflect the use of an alternative test, a risky proposition for any school. A drop in the rankings would in turn risk alumni donations, employer willingness to hire graduates and a number of other "network goods" connected to a law school's status in the rankings.[24] Taken together, these costs go a long way toward explaining why law schools wring their hands about the disparate impact that the LSAT has on the racial diversity of its matriculants, but do not abandon or replace the test.

A third type of switching cost, the political switching cost, is most significant in the kind of institutional change that requires political machinery to make the change. Political costs stand in the way of many potential reforms that might reduce structural racial inequality, and political costs often go hand in hand with economic costs for one particular group. In the context of public goods financing, political costs help to explain why school funding and other public goods financing continue to rely on local wealth, despite the fact that this relationship makes racial inequality self-reinforcing.

Voters are a big part of the narrative of switching costs in the public goods context. Economist William Fischel writes about the "homevoter," who drives political decision making at the local level, particularly when it comes to local government, land use, and school financing. A stockholder controls corporate decision making and focuses almost exclusively on the effect of decisions on stock price. Likewise, the homevoter judges politics through a narrow lens: the effect of choices on the value of his home. Politicians are often quite unlikely to be able to pay the political cost of angering the homevoter by adopting reforms that would lower the homevoter's property values.[25]

Among other programs, homevoters have blocked many kinds of inclusionary zoning programs that require developers to build low-income housing as the price for getting a zoning permit. Homevoters have also blocked judicial efforts to centralize school financing at the level of the state. When the California Supreme Court, in *Serrano v. Priest* (1971), required centralized funding for school districts in order to address widespread economic and racial disparity, homevoters reacted by passing Proposition 13, which limited the amount of property tax that the state could impose to raise funds for centralized school funding.[26] Because homevoters had organized as a potent political bloc in response to their economic switching costs, they effectively shut down the revenue source that the California legislature had targeted to fund centralized school finance.[27]

It is important to reiterate that these switching costs operate quite independently of racial animus. Homevoters oppose inclusionary zoning not because they have an irrational hostility toward blacks and Latinos, but because black and Latino neighbors are less wealthy and will drag property values down. Law schools are reluctant to switch to a less exclusionary admissions program because structurally they would have to redesign much of their bureaucratic arrangements and because they would risk a tumble in the rankings. These switching costs are what lock in racial disparity, even in the absence of ongoing intentional discrimination.

Critical Thresholds

Lock-in dynamics display another key feature that helps to explain why racial disparities persist. Lock-in dynamics often exhibit something called a critical threshold, a sort of dividing line that separates a system that reproduces racial inequality from one that eventually eliminates inequality.

Dynamic systems often display critical thresholds that separate different states of the system. The boiling point, for instance, separates water from steam; the freezing point separates water from ice. Likewise, the dynamics of wealth also display a critical point that some scholars call the Micawber threshold, after the eternally destitute but forever cheery character in the Dickens novel, *David Copperfield*. This threshold also separates qualitatively different states or categories of family wealth.

Above the Micawber threshold, families are upwardly mobile. They have sufficient assets for positive feedback loops to push the family's wealth upward on the ladder to success. Below the threshold, families' assets put them in survival mode, and their disadvantage creates further disadvantage, pushing a family down the chute toward poverty. These are the chronically poor.[28]

Empirical research demonstrates that people's positions either below or above the Micawber threshold can be tied to race. In the US, blacks are far more likely to be downwardly mobile or trapped in poverty than are whites, most likely because their asset levels are low owing to historic discrimination.[29] Likewise, in South Africa, black households that have fallen below a threshold level of income about twice the poverty line consistently will spiral down the chute until they reach a level at about 90 percent of the poverty line.[30]

Social networks also display critical thresholds that appear to separate the lucky from the not so lucky. Job referral networks appear to have a critical density—how many links a person has to potential references.[31] Above the magic number, people in the network will almost certainly be referred for employment. Below the threshold number, the probability that someone will find work through the network drops dramatically to zero. This critical threshold might help to explain the formation of the hyperghetto.

We also see evidence of a critical threshold in the link between income and public education. In one evolutionary path, if the population's income falls below the critical threshold, the population then begins to invest too little in education because people can't afford it. This path produces progressively lower income until the system reaches equilibrium. In the other path, where the population's income exceeds some critical threshold, income begins to grow ever more quickly, because people can afford to invest in schooling, which increases the population's income even more.[32]

Critical thresholds are important to understanding lock-in, because they show how small racialized differences—differences in assets, in network links, in public spending on education—can split the country into the haves and have-nots on the basis of race and class. The dynamics of becoming wealthy can send families of color down the chute to poverty, even after they have worked hard to save and acquire assets.

More generally, this chapter has demonstrated that racial disparity may now be fixed and unchanging, in the absence of some dramatic government intervention. We may well have passed an important point on the evolutionary time line of our country's racial arrangements, when the cost of switching to integrated networks and institutions has now become prohibitive. If economic, structural, social, and political costs have become too high, integration may be more unattainable than it was just after civil rights legislation was passed. Racial disparities might be getting a lot worse over time instead of getting better.

It might also be worth noting that locking in racial inequality may not have required all that much racial discrimination to begin with. Tipping the urn of our racial landscape toward white dominance might have required only a small amount of cartel conduct at the beginning, during a critical window of time, to achieve critical levels of segregation. If this is true, then it will come as no surprise that hundreds of years of slavery and Jim Crow have affected contemporary levels of inequality. As the next chapter explores in more detail, racial disparity might now persist over time, even in the absence of ongoing intentional exclusion.

Reframing Race

How the Lock-In Model Helps Us to Think in
New Ways about Racial Inequality

In 1989, the US Supreme Court issued its decision in what would turn out to be one of the Court's seminal affirmative action cases, *City of Richmond v. J.A. Croson Co* (1989).[1] The city of Richmond, Virginia had adopted a program that reserved 30 percent of the dollar amount of any contract for minority-owned construction companies.[2] A white-owned company challenged the program in court, arguing that it violated the owner's right to equal protection. The Court declared the set-aside program illegal, finding that the goal of remedying societal discrimination could not justify the quota imposed by the city. In the Court's view, it didn't matter that blacks historically had been excluded from trade unions and apprenticeship programs; "an amorphous claim that there has been past discrimination in a particular industry cannot justify the use of an unyielding racial quota."[3]

The Court's opinion did note at the outset that Richmond had had a sorry history when it came to black participation in the construction industry. In 1983, Richmond's principal construction trade association, the Associated General Contractors, had not a single black member— not one.[4] And, as the appellant's brief noted, the lack of a black member was all the more striking when one considered that AGC had over six hundred members in Richmond, and that nationally its members performed over 80 percent of all construction work in the country. Of course, none of the other major construction trade associations in the Richmond area had any black members at the time either. Not surprisingly, an extremely small number of the city's prime contracts were awarded to minority-owned construction companies: less than 1 percent, over a five-year period.[5]

Even so, the Court found the city's plan to remedy past discrimination to be too amorphous for several reasons. Most importantly, the city had made no specific factual findings of past historical discrimination in Richmond's construction industry. Richmond's primary proof had been to point out the dramatic statistical disparity between the number of people of color in Richmond (50 percent) and the percentage of contracts being awarded to minority-owned businesses (0.67 percent).[6] But the Court did not consider the statistical generalization to be proof that discrimination existed in the industry.

Indeed, the Court noted that the statistical disparity might actually be traced to many different sources: past discrimination in education and economic opportunity, or perhaps the differing career choices of blacks and whites. Perhaps most importantly, the Court found that the city could not prove how many black construction companies might have existed, or gotten contracts, if whites had not historically discriminated.[7]

In focusing on the need for such "but for" proof, the Court adopted the view that an affirmative action program could be justified only if it were narrowly circumscribed to address recent discrimination that could be directly tied to existing racial disparities in the labor force. In the Court's view, to justify a set-aside on the basis of "amorphous" claims of past discrimination in the industry would be to justify too much in the way of reverse discrimination, and for too long.

What might the Court's reasoning have looked like if it had embraced a lock-in model of persistent discrimination? First, the Court might have framed the City's effort to remedy discrimination less as compensation for past intentional discrimination and more as a focused effort to remedy present inequality that had become locked in owing to early historical discrimination.

In that vein, the Court might have paid much more attention to the evidence of very bad cartel behavior by whites early in the history of Richmond's construction industry. The briefs in the case fairly brimmed with evidence of historical cartel behavior, not just in Richmond but also in the national construction industry. Whites had collectively evicted blacks after the Civil War from their positions as skilled craft workers. They had brazenly excluded blacks from skilled construction trade unions, training programs, and trade associations. They had hired blacks only for relatively unskilled positions and had conspired to prevent black construction workers from following the traditional path from laborer to entrepreneur. The Court might have understood such conduct not just as irrational, but as unfair conduct designed to give whites a competitive leg up in the construction industry.

Second, the Court might have recognized, as Congress had done when it passed Title VII, that race-neutral processes like bonding requirements could extend the impact of historical exclusion.[8] For example, the Court might have recognized that black-owned construction companies can find it hard to meet capital or bonding requirements because they have entered the industry relatively later in the game, and have less experience to reassure bonding companies or banks.

Likewise, the Court might have acknowledged that these companies' poor performance in the frequent informal preselection process might well have been tied to the more marginalized location of the companies in professional social networks. Indeed, as Congress had recognized, and as the appellant brief made clear, capital and bonding requirements and preselection requirements were precisely the sort of processes that reward first-movers who unfairly have achieved seniority in an industry.

In fact, in its decision, the Court had recognized the kinds of historic discrimination described here, but never tied that discrimination to contemporary outcomes. The Court could have described that earlier discrimination not as amorphous and attenuated, but as something perhaps even quantifiably connected to struggles with bonding and capital requirements, marketability, and the like.

Finally, the Court might have looked at the 30 percent set-aside as an antitrust-style remedy, needed to equalize competition by dismantling the feedback loop that keeps black companies from catching up. Certainly, courts have required much of incumbent companies when making sure that competitors have access to networks and resources in the wake of an antitrust ruling. The Court could have justified the 30 percent set-aside in the same way, as a corrective measure that would allow the new competitors to develop their own adequate track records, their access to capital, their entry into professional networks, and their access to other resources that whites had monopolized in Richmond for so long.

This chapter suggests that the lock-in model can offer several new ways of thinking about persistent racial inequality that run contrary to conventional thinking. First, racial inequality can be "path dependent."[9] In path dependent processes like our Polya urn, history plays a central role in explaining outcomes. Even relatively small historical events like a typing contest—let alone big historical events like hundreds of years of exclusion—can ultimately help to determine where competitors can end up. Although many conservative commentators insist that contemporary outcomes are unrelated to past history, the lock-in model suggests that history likely plays an important role in contemporary racial differences.

Second, the model proposes that racial inequality is automatic and self-reinforcing, and might continue indefinitely, even in the absence of intentional discrimination. As we discussed in the first chapter, economists like Gary Becker have suggested that market forces will weed out discriminators because discrimination is expensive and imposes a competitive disadvantage. The lock-in model suggests that, far from helping, market competition actually reinforces historical inequality because discrimination pays off.

Third, the lock-in model suggests that self-reinforcing racial disparity might well be economically inefficient. Standard economic theory teaches that a competitive market efficiently allocates resources based on people's tastes and preferences. The lock-in model suggests, however, that segregated markets are potentially (and actually) inefficient, and that we are losing significant potential productivity by continuing on the current path.

The following discussion considers each of these new ways of thinking about inequality in much more detail.

History (and Context) Matter

Given the magnitude of Jim Crow and slavery, finding a connection between historical exclusion and contemporary racial disparity would seem relatively uncontroversial for many scholars. For years, economic historians have been saying as much. Whites systematically drove particular groups of people out of key markets—labor, education, housing, and political markets. How could such pervasive and long-lasting exclusion not be connected in some way to contemporary disparity?

Resisting that intuition, a number of commentators have argued that history doesn't matter, or that it matters much less than culture, in explaining contemporary racial differences. Conservative scholars like Stephen and Abigail Thernstrom have argued, for example, that our country's racial history is firmly behind us, and the inferior culture of blacks and Latinos really is to blame for persistent racial gaps in income, education and housing.[10] Like the Thernstroms, the Court in *Croson* also implicitly suggested that culture might be to blame, speculating that blacks might be "disproportionately attracted" to industries other than construction.[11] Other scholars have suggested that racialized "cultural" differences in investment and savings can explain racial gaps in wealth.[12] And a number of scholars have argued that racialized differences in social norms and attitudes about education, work, achievement, child rearing, and family structure are more directly responsible for persistent racial disparity.[13]

In contrast, the lock-in model proposes that Jim Crow and slavery played a central role in explaining contemporary racial differences. In particular, the lock-in model argues that slavery and Jim Crow gave whites a significant and self-reproducing unfair advantage early in the game, and that advantage now reproduces itself from generation to generation.

How did these early historical events create today's racial arrangements? By setting up the initial conditions—a sort of foundational template—for subsequent developments. Evolutionary biologists like Stephen Jay Gould argue that big environmental changes will chart a particular path for subsequent evolution, because those dramatic events shape the direction of ordinary evolutionary processes.[14] A flood reshapes the direction of the river, for example, and subsequent evolution proceeds from that point forward. In path-dependent systems, what happens in the past plays a very big role in shaping what happens in the future.

In the story of contemporary historical inequality, the history of slavery and Jim Crow played a central role. It is worth noting at the outset that with regard to slavery and Jim Crow, the key historical events were not nearly as minor as a random typing contest early in the typewriter industry's development. Slavery and Jim Crow are quite major events, and quite long-lasting ones, and the idea that they would continue to explain contemporary disparities seems more than just plausible but probable.

Indeed, centuries-long historical exclusion of black construction workers would mean that black-owned companies necessarily would have shorter track records, thinner professional networks, and a harder time satisfying capital and bonding requirements. On the other hand, white companies would have benefited, as the story about shop classes in Chapter 6 demonstrates. Would it be all that irrational for black residents of Richmond to stay clear of the construction industry given its early history?

Indeed, historians and other scholars have documented that, as a more general matter, slavery and Jim Crow segregation have paved the way to contemporary inequality. For example, legal scholar Richard Ford has suggested that segregation created the original foundation on which contemporary housing patterns were then built. State-sponsored and private segregation created separate white neighborhoods with corresponding benefits: neighbors with higher incomes, larger homes and bigger properties, more privately financed amenities, lower taxes for publicly financed amenities, better public schools, and social networks that offered a neighbor more access to wealth and power.[15]

Segregation also put together poorer people of color in neighborhoods with smaller homes, fewer amenities, higher taxes, poorly funded public schools and social networks, and neighbors who were frequently under or unemployed. As Ford points out, those initial arrangements became self-reinforcing over time. Neighborhoods with wealth produced children with higher incomes and better public services, and neighborhoods that began with an initial disadvantage reproduced that disadvantage. As Chapter 3 outlines, those early historical events charted a particular path for competition in housing markets, giving an initial, and persistent, advantage to whites.

Likewise, segregation in politics also played a defining role in the subsequent evolution of Southern politics. Disenfranchisement laws dramatically reduced voter turnout and party competition. White primaries consolidated white power in organized political networks that were well funded. These laws boosted white political power for decades to come.[16] In many ways, these legal changes were rigid enough to reshape the political landscape entirely, in a path-dependent way.

The lock-in model also proposes that context matters, and in particular, a person's membership in a racial group matters. Conventional economic thinking treats each person's economic welfare as autonomous and independent of their membership in groups or their interactions with other people. In standard models, rational actors make decisions on the basis of their preferences and don't incorporate others' decisions or preferences into their decision making.

In contrast, the lock-in model suggests that people's interactions with each other and with their institutions—their families, neighborhoods, social networks, workplaces, local governments—constrain and shape their preferences and choices.[17] For example, a person's ability to get a job depends not just on her qualifications and labor supply and demand, but on the kinds of jobs her network and community connections have. Owing to history, her racial identity and that of her network shapes whether or not her network has the kinds of jobs that pay high wages and offer the opportunity for advancement.

Likewise, a student's level of education depends not just on her effort and ability but also on those of her classmates, the level of the school's financing, and the property tax base of her neighborhood. And given the country's history, her racial identity strongly correlates with school financing levels, property tax bases, and achievement levels at the school. This is as true today as it was in the early twentieth century, when the quality of the education that Latinos could get was determined by their racial identity.

Group interaction also helps to explain how white cartel members shaped each other's preferences. White real estate brokers and homeowners' associations strongly influenced the decision of their members to exclude blacks from housing markets. Texas political parties agreed among themselves to keep black voters off the rolls. White labor unions mobilized to evict black workers from skilled positions in railroad yards of the Midwest. For much of the twentieth century, these racial group effects strongly shaped a person's choices about how to treat in-group and out-group members.

Self-Reinforcing Inequality and Inflexibility

The lock-in model changes our thinking about persistent racial inequality in a second way. The model focuses on the way in which inequality reinforces itself, from generation to generation, and the way in which inequality becomes rigid and inflexible, locked in by market forces.

Here again, the dynamics of the model run contrary to conventional economic theory. As discussed in more detail in Chapter 1, economists famously have argued that in the long run, market competition should drive out discrimination. Discrimination costs employers money because they pay higher wages when their supply of workers is smaller, or they earn less profit when their workforce is less productive. In theory, those firms that do not discriminate will eventually outcompete those that do.[18] Discriminating firms will either adopt their more successful competitors' strategy and stop discriminating, or be driven out by market competition.

The lock-in model suggests, however, that markets are often characterized not by competition but by collective action and monopolization. For example, as Chapter 1 described, members of the Kenwood Property Owners' Association in Chicago agreed that they would not sell to black buyers, creating a dual housing market and the possibility of monopoly profits for whites. In particular, whites monopolized access to superior housing stock, wealthier neighbors, and better public amenities. Whatever whites might have sacrificed in the way of a smaller pool of people to sell to, they more than gained back in higher property values, higher incomes, and better public goods. Thus, because collective discrimination paid off handsomely, market forces actually reproduced inequality, rather than pushed against it.

The lock-in model also (and perhaps most importantly) highlights the inflexibility of the market, once advantage becomes locked in.[19] Switching costs make it very unlikely that consumers can move to another product once it has captured market dominance. Likewise, switching costs make it highly unlikely that social processes—law school admissions, job referral networks, public goods financing—can be restructured in a way that makes them less exclusionary. A market characterized by cartel conduct and switching costs is quite unlikely to drive out racial inequality.

Locked In: The Inefficiency of Segregation

The lock-in model produces a third very important insight. Racial segregation—in social networks, neighborhoods, job categories—is potentially inefficient. In a technology market characterized by increasing returns, consumers might choose a technology not because the technology is any more innovative, but because other people have chosen it. Some commentators argue, for example, that Betamax is technically superior to VHS and that the market locked in the less efficient technology because of its earlier success.[20] If this is true, then the market has become locked into the technologically inferior product.

Of course, the debate about efficiency is a bit more complicated than that. VHS isn't necessarily less efficient just because it was the victor in an increasing returns market. In other circumstances, self-reinforcing effects might actually lock in the advantage of the better, more innovative alternative. But the lock-in model suggests that we can't rely on market dominance to tell us whether the technology is more innovative or intrinsically better. Because earlier success (and not just better technology) determines market success in an increasing market, it's hard to say what is and isn't more efficient. For example, economists have argued that geographically (or racially) segregating high-skill workers from low-skill workers can potentially be inefficient, because low-skill workers are unable to educate each other; or efficient, because high-skill workers will educate each other.[21] The question can only be resolved by determining empirically which effect is greater than the other.

Likewise, racially segregated markets—job markets, education markets, housing markets—might well be efficient. But there is far more reason to think them inefficient. Spillovers from wealthy neighbors can benefit wealthy whites. But spillovers among poor neighbors in segregated neighborhoods likely increase the costs of education, housing or jobs on the other side of the ledger. Segregation might well produce a net loss: the benefits of lowered costs to the wealthier, white community might be more than outweighed by the increased costs associated with poor, racially segregated communities.[22]

Are racially segregated markets actually inefficient? Empirical research suggests that they are, in many circumstances. Economists find that racial segregation imposes significant costs in the form of more expensive education and lost income for black residents of inner-city ghettos. At the same time, segregation appears to provide few if any benefits for whites in terms of less expensive education and higher income for those in wealthier neighborhoods.[23] Scholars estimate that reducing segregation by one standard deviation would eliminate one-third of black/white differences in income and education. Depending on the size of the disadvantaged group, reducing segregation can increase efficiency.[24]

Segregation is much more likely to be inefficient if one considers the longer term, as opposed to short-run costs and benefits. Integrating low- and high-skill in the same classroom helps to modernize a city's workforce toward higher-skilled services, as low-skilled workers benefit from mixing with high-skilled workers. But as is true with regard to most institutional decision making, policy makers orient their decision making toward short-term results rather than long-term payoffs.

There is some evidence to suggest that racial segregation might be efficient on some measures. One line of argument suggests that segregation might be efficient because it promotes intercommunity trust. Political scientist Robert Putnam most famously has documented that racial differences can often hinder people's ability to develop relationships of trust and collaborative spirit.[25] In general, Putnam's research confirmed the findings of a number of other studies—that racial difference and trust are negatively correlated. Putnam's research suggests more bad news: according to his data, people who live in a racially diverse area trusted people of another race less *and* were also less trusting of people of their own race. Putnam interpreted his data to mean that diversity caused people to hunker down and to become more socially isolated.

But Putnam himself argues that in the long run, integrated communities are more efficient. As members of groups come together under a common identity, intergroup trust can facilitate broader cooperation. Putnam and other scholars argue that over time, deliberate policies that create a "new more capacious sense of 'we'" can ameliorate and even reverse the loss in trust that racial difference creates.[26]

The Antitrust Analogy

The lock-in model also changes the way we think about racial inequality by suggesting that antitrust might be an appropriate framework for thinking about racial inequality. In this framework, whites weren't just unfair for irrational reasons—they acted as a monopoly to gain competitive advantage. In that vein, antidiscrimination remedies aren't just about improving social justice. Such remedies are also about leveling the economic playing field and ensuring free and open competition.

Describing racial exclusion as anticompetitive conduct is not entirely new. Indeed, in at least one federal case, plaintiffs framed their claims of racial discrimination as antitrust claims. In *Organization of Minority Vendors v. Illinois Gulf Central Railroad* (1983), plaintiffs wanted to enforce the requirements of an affirmative action program that required railroads to use minority-owned suppliers.[27] The minority organization argued that white long-time suppliers had anticompetitively conspired with the Illinois Gulf Central Railroad to fake their status as minority-owned, in order to exclude real minority-owned businesses from any contracts.

Amazingly, the Illinois federal trial court bought the argument, and ruled that plaintiffs had a valid antitrust claim. The court focused mostly on the collective action nature of the white boycott. In the court's view, plaintiffs had demonstrated that they'd suffered economic injury from the defendant's anticompetitive action.

Describing racial discrimination as anticompetitive, and antidiscrimination as antitrust changes the way we think about racial discrimination and racial disparity. First, by emphasizing the idea of market competition, the model highlights the economic costs and historical benefits of racial discrimination. Our common understanding of racism has tended to focus much more on the so-called irrational motivations of animus. We have paid far less attention to the economic motivations of historical actors. The antitrust analogy emphasizes that whites profited handsomely from exclusion and segregation during Jim Crow and slavery.

More specifically, whites unfairly monopolized the best neighborhoods, the most well-funded schools, the highest-paying workplaces, and the most powerful political organizations. They used coercion and violence to be able to live in exclusive neighborhoods with the wealthiest neighbors, in the best houses. They colluded to enjoy the most prestigious, high-paying jobs with the most opportunity for advancement. They created cartels to give them disproportionate political power. Unfair discrimination paid off in very tangible ways. Recall that according to Lester Thurow, whites received a $15.5 billion payoff (and that was just at the outset) from their discriminatory behavior.[28]

In addition, the antitrust analogy highlights the unfairness of white advantage. Whites used the same anticompetitive tactics that market cartels traditionally use—economic coercion, violence, and harassment—to exclude people of color from key markets. Whites hobbled their competitors to get ahead of them in the race. In more formal economic terms, they externalized or displaced the cost of their profits by exploiting other people.

 Scholars like Dalton Conley have made the very strong argument from social justice that regardless of unfairness, and regardless of the inequality between black and white, between the have and the have-nots, we ought to do as much as we can to eliminate racialized poverty. But for those who oppose redistribution, the antitrust analogy functions quite effectively as an internal critique. It suggests that whites stacked the decks in their own favor, by rigging the rules of the game.

Third and finally, thinking of antidiscrimination in terms of antitrust helps to justify the more radical nature and scale of some of the remedies discussed in the next chapter—like a trust fund for every child of color whose parents are not wealthy. In the antitrust world, on several notable occasions courts have ordered complete industry restructuring. Quite famously, courts ordered the dismantling of long-standing corporate giants, in the case of *Standard Oil of New Jersey v. US* (1911), and divestiture in *US v. AT&T* (1982).[29]

Likewise, in the Department of Justice's case against Microsoft, the Court seriously considered the proposed remedy of breaking up the company.[30] In asking the federal court to dismantle Microsoft, the department argued that restoring competition in the operating systems market required significant and dramatic legal intervention, in order to eliminate the barrier to entry created by increasing returns. Eliminating positive feedback loops like wealth, neighborhood, and social network processes described in earlier chapters likely will require dramatic legal intervention, to restructure the market so that competition might be fair. The next chapter explores ways to dismantle these feedback loops, by way of interventions both dramatic and ordinary.

10

Unlocking Lock-In

Some General Observations (and One or Two Suggestions) on Dismantling Lock-In

In 2010, sociologists Darrick Hamilton and William Darity, Jr. proposed a bold policy to close the black and Latino wealth gap: baby bonds. If wealthy white families gave their kids a head start by putting them through college and giving them a down payment on a house, then the government could give wealth-poor families of color their own head start through children's trust funds. In particular, the government could provide asset-poor children a sum of money at birth, a "baby bond," in a guaranteed growth rate account, that would be enough to provide $50,000 or $60,000 for kids when they turned eighteen. Parents could put in additional funds that the government would match. The baby bond money would be held in federally managed investment, and young adults could withdraw the money for purposes of education, home purchases or retirement.[1]

To justify baby bonds, the authors pointed to much of the history recounted here in earlier chapters—the history of slavery, Jim Crow laws, the failure of government to redistribute property after the Civil War, redlining, and enforcement of restrictive covenants. To keep the program constitutional, the authors proposed that the program be based on wealth rather than income, noting of course the significant correlation between race and wealth. And to satisfy the skeptics who might have argued that such a program wasn't feasible, Hamilton and Darity pointed to the United Kingdom's equally bold (but much smaller scale) policy of providing every child born in the UK with a "trust fund"—£500 per child, and £1,000 for needy children—with additional installments when the child turned seven.[2]

The idea behind baby bonds was simple—to provide young adults starting out with the kind of foundational trust fund wealth to which whites have historically significantly more access. If a young adult had money in the bank for a college tuition, a down payment for buying a house, or other wealth-generating activities, she could begin her adult life with the same sort of financial advantage that whites get more often from their parents. If it takes money to make money, then baby bonds would give families of color the kind of head start they needed to make the kind of cumulative wealth that whites had been earning for generations. A remedy like baby bonds would work because it would address the kinds of feedback loops we have been discussing.

This chapter explores the theoretical question of whether lock-in can be remedied. The argument from previous chapters has been that structural racial inequality is locked in because switching costs are quite high, and in fact might be too high to expect people to pay. This chapter focuses less on specific policy prescriptions, and more on general ideas about how to dismantle feedback loops. For example, we will investigate policy reforms like baby bonds as a way to more generally explore the theory behind dismantling or hijacking the feedback loops that reproduce inequality. As well, we will consider the way in which switching costs tend to lurk behind every potentially promising idea.

We will first consider the possibility that shifting social norms might play a role in lowering switching costs. We will then consider three approaches to dealing with feedback loops—limiting them, integrating them, or replicating them for communities of color.

Social Norms?

Much of switching costs comes from the social norms that structure our everyday social arrangements. Feedback loops are generated in the everyday choices that people take for granted, like referring friends for jobs, giving financial assistance to one's children, or choosing neighborhoods on the basis of ability to pay. Policy makers will have a very hard time restructuring those processes because they are so deeply entrenched in the way we do business. For this reason, we may, in fact, be locked in.

But locked-in systems, even those that involve processes with big switching costs, can sometimes be dismantled if policy makers can shift social norms to change the equation. Consider an example from the field of technology: the competition between electric cars and gasoline-powered cars. Drivers can refuel their gas-powered cars easily by buying gas via a readily available network of gas stations. In comparison, electric cars must be recharged, and the battery storage capacity for such cars was, at least until recently, quite small. The switching costs of moving from convenient gas stations to frequent recharging and limited distance driving seemed insurmountable. Until a few years ago, finding investors to finance research into battery storage proved quite difficult, given the lack of a ready-made market for electric cars that could compete with gas-powered cars.

But economists predicted, quite accurately as it turns out, that policy makers could break the complete lock-in for gasoline powered cars with the right norms-based approach. Back in the mid-1990s, a small number of economists suggested that consumers could be persuaded to gradually shift to electric cars by both imposing regulatory requirements and also by generating some sort of change in social norms about driving big gas-guzzling cars, via advertising and role modeling by public figures.[3]

Beginning with upper middle-class consumers, social norms around the environment shifted quite suddenly, in the space of a decade. Suddenly, driving a Hummer became affirmatively uncool, and the behemoth car became the poster-child for poor fuel economy. At the same time, driving fuel-saving cars like the Toyota Prius became desirable, even fashionable. Investments in electric car research began to pick up steam and at some point, the unthinkable became thinkable—electric cars on the market. Although electric cars have yet to take off, a number of carmakers have put electric cars on the market, a move that would have been completely unthinkable ten years ago.

Why would making environmental conservation cool enable a shift toward electric cars? Switching costs—the availability of gas stations relative to recharging options, coupled with the geeky image of electric cars—created lock-in for gas-powered cars. But once consumer attitudes toward fuel conservation shifted, switching costs in effect went down because they were offset by the benefits of being cool, or perhaps more accurately, the costs of being uncool. Once it was uncool to drive gas guzzlers, people were more likely to pay the switching costs to drive fuel-saving cars, including electric.[4]

So what implications does the electric car story have for our lock-in model? Could policy makers mobilize social norms to persuade people to restructure how they allocate resources among family, neighborhood, social, and workplace networks? There is some reason to think so. We have ample evidence now that social norms that connect to inequality are quite malleable. In late 2011, the Occupy Wall Street movement and other protests based on class inequality took to the streets in over 80 countries and 950 cities. Many political candidates in the 2012 elections have focused on the widening gap between rich and poor. Where inequality was relatively routine and uncontroversial in the Gilded Age and again in the 1980s and 1990s, citizen norms have shifted somewhat to favor a less unequal social distribution.[5]

What if the energy that motivates protest against class-based inequality were mobilized against the kinds of racial disparities we have been discussing—wealth, housing, education, health care, and political participation? Would whites voluntarily restructure their family, neighborhood, and social networks, once they understood the effects of doing so? Would they voluntarily pay to finance baby bonds? Could policy makers shift ideas about racial inequality the way they shifted ideas about electric cars? Given that most of the modern public conversation about race focuses on intentional discrimination, it is hard to imagine at present a national conversation about structural processes of the sort this book describes.

Beyond vague questions about social norms, what broader implications about remedy can we draw from our theoretical descriptions of lock-in? Given the way that inequality gets locked in, dismantling lock-in might take one of three forms: (1) limit white feedback loops in some way, so that whites don't continue to get ahead faster than people of color; (2) integrate the feedback loop, so that communities of color can benefit from the same processes that reproduce white advantage; and (3) generate a parallel loop (if none exists) for communities of color, so that they can harness the same processes on their own behalf from which whites now benefit. Baby bonds might be an example of this approach. We will discuss each theoretical category of remedy in turn.

Limit the Loop

Proposals to limit feedback loops might focus on limiting the benefits that whites enjoy from feedback loops, or taxing those benefits to redistribute the wealth toward communities of color. Whites enjoy wealth, job referrals, better public goods, and other benefits by way of feedback loops that reproduce earlier inequality generated by intentional discrimination. Limiting the loops for some period of time in order to reduce that unfair advantage might be one way to reduce inequality.

The most radical of such proposals could tax the benefits that whites enjoy from their feedback loops and redistribute the resulting wealth to communities of color. For example, legal scholar Roberto Unger has proposed that we dramatically increase inheritance and estate taxes to limit the benefits that the "haves" get from family inheritance, but "have-nots" don't enjoy. Unger argues that we could use the revenue generated by these taxes to provide the kind of social support that families usually provide in a capitalist system. Unger's proposal really seeks to radically restructure social arrangements, away from family as the primary source of inheritance and more toward society in general. As Unger puts it, "social inheritance for all would generally replace family inheritance for the few."[6]

Aggressive inheritance and estate taxes might begin to dismantle the feedback loops of family transmission of wealth that Chapter 4 identifies as a primary engine of locked-in racial inequality. To further refine the program's aim at race, policy makers could impose inheritance and estate taxes on those mechanisms of transmission that produce the biggest racial gaps—not just inheritance, but specially targeting family assistance with tuition and down payments on purchases of a house, particularly those homes that are purchased as second homes or for investment purposes. The funds generated from such significant taxes could be used to finance society-based transmission of wealth, like baby bonds or children's trust funds.

Likewise, policy makers could limit feedback loops in job referrals. To limit the impact of network benefits to whites, policy makers could ban informal network hiring in all-white institutions, at least until the institution had amassed a critical mass of workers of color on site. Once the institution had a critical mass, it could begin again to use informal networks. With a diverse workforce to use as a seed group, network hiring could begin to help further diversify the institution.

Currently, the Equal Employment Opportunity Commission (EEOC) discourages word-of-mouth hiring. Compliance regulations advise employers of the potential hazards of network hiring: "While word-of-mouth recruiting in a racially diverse workforce can be an effective way to promote diversity, the same method of recruiting in a nondiverse workforce is a barrier to equal employment opportunity if it does not create applicant pools that reflect the diversity in the qualified labor market."[7] A stronger ban on network hiring that pegs use of the method to the diversity of the employee population might more narrowly limit white advantage from network referrals.

The aforementioned remedies work by preventing feedback loops from continuing to make the white rich richer, so to speak. But their primary disadvantage is quite obvious. Politically, whites are likely to fiercely resist policy reform that equalizes downward by limiting white benefits (or redistributing them). Recent survey data by the Pew Research Center indicates that only a third of Americans surveyed favored doing anything that would affect material redistribution, including preferential treatment, to improve the position of minorities; in 2012, 62 percent of blacks and 59 percent of Latinos agreed with race-based preferential treatment, but only 22 percent of whites did. Results were quite polarized by party affiliation and income to a lesser degree.[8] Although failure to support preferential treatment based on race does not necessarily mean people would resist strategies to limit the loop, to the extent that such strategies actually limit the accumulation of white advantage, there is reason to think that this data is instructive.

Barring a shift in social norms of the kind described above, political switching costs are likely to make these kinds of remedies unlikely. What other remedies might address the relevant feedback loops?

Integrate the Loop

As the saying goes, "if you can't beat 'em, join 'em." Integrating people of color into existing feedback loops might help to equalize or otherwise diminish locked-in inequality. Feedback loops create disproportionate advantage for whites because the loops tend to distribute opportunity and resources to people of the same race. Because people are more likely to socially connect to others of the same race ("homophily"), social networks tend to be racially homogenous. Likewise, family wealth loops are usually same-race loops.

Integrating a loop would mean adding people of color as participants into those family, social network, neighborhood and workplace processes that have benefitted whites. But if limiting the loop is a tough political sell, integration would be more so. Policy makers have been trying for years to integrate workplaces and neighborhoods, with little success, in large part because white flight is always the next step—to the suburbs, to create another exclusive social network, to open another private school. To effectively integrate the most wealth-enhancing feedback loops—families, neighborhoods, and social networks—means limiting the opportunity for white flight.

How might we integrate professional and social networks in a way that limits or discourages white flight? Some scholars have suggested that integrating online networks might be easier than off-line networks, so to speak. Professional online networks like LinkedIn and Ryze offer the opportunity to professionally (and socially) network online. These digital networks, or others like them, potentially might offer minority job applicants a way to break into business networks, to improve their flow of information and increase their likelihood of success. One could imagine requiring all-white firms to use integrated or minority professional online networks for job hiring, at least until a sufficiently large number of employees were nonwhite.

Limiting white flight likely would still be an issue. To make online networks small enough and of high enough quality to be useful, network sponsors usually limit membership in some way—for example, by requiring a person to be invited by existing members to join the network.[9] Indeed, at least one commentator has remarked that on-line networks work mostly to deepen the advantage of an already advantaged group.[10] So long as network value is connected to the resources of network members, whites will likely continue to seek out ways to increase the exclusivity of their networks.

Online networks also face the digital divide problem—the problem that people of color are less likely to have or use computers than whites. But recent surveys indicate that the digital divide between whites and people of color is closing very rapidly, and that black and Latino teens spend more time online in chat rooms than do white teens.[11] Filipinos and other groups have used social networks to create economic relationships and develop niche positions or "ethnic economies."[12] Online networks may well become a key element in strategies to improve the economic position of communities of color.

What about integrating networks via special invitation from willing members? The idea here is that by piggybacking off of a successful network member's connections, the more junior network member can get access to higher-quality network resources. Practically speaking, mentorship programs work on the idea that following around a successful agent gives the mentee an opportunity to see how an expert does her work as well as the chance to meet the people the mentor knows. With a recommendation from the mentor, the mentee has even more access to the mentor's social network, because the recommendation serves as a signal that the mentee is of high quality on whatever measure of quality the network prizes.

Of course, mentorship programs cannot just rely on informal social networks to put mentees of color together with white mentors. Programs that are deliberately cross-racial might be one way to give people of color entry into what otherwise are mostly white networks of access. Of course, research indicates that cross-racial mentorships are frequently the most difficult to create effectively, for the same reasons that explain why they don't form naturally.[13]

Neighborhood feedback loops might be a bit easier to integrate. Government can redraw legal jurisdictional boundaries to promote integration at the regional level, when segregation persists at the neighborhood or community level. Regional approaches to public education, transportation, jobs, and business development have seen some success in forcing wealthier white communities to bear their fair share of the social burden. Cities like Seattle, Minneapolis, and Portland (not necessarily the most diverse cities in the country, though more than most people guess) have adopted regional approaches to taxing and spending for public goods.

Most often, a regional approach to urban and suburban planning takes place in two steps. In the first step, communities in the region are asked to equitably share the costs of development. In the second step, communities move to more fairly share the benefits of concentrated wealth and neighborhood effects that improve quality of life. Those who benefit from government infrastructure can be made to share those benefits with low-income residents.

Regional approaches have worked in some places. In Minneapolis, for example, the government moved to share property tax-bases among regional municipalities and districts, in accordance with the area's commercial and industrial wealth.[14] Poorer governments in the region got a bigger share of the resources from property tax-base sharing to fund housing and redevelopment. Tax-base sharing worked because it helped to create more equity in public services, and perhaps more importantly, cut down on the tendency to zone for purposes of hoarding tax-base wealth.

Zoning law can also be restructured to try to integrate the loop. Inclusionary zoning requires the benefits of wealthy neighbors and well-funded public goods be shared more equitably. Inclusionary zoning takes many forms, but the basic idea is that developers are not permitted to develop a neighborhood unless they provide housing for low-income families. Some municipalities have created set-asides for affordable housing, either by way of a mandatory requirement or via a point bonus in a point-based permit program. The most successful inclusionary zoning programs have included a mandatory requirement that operates regardless of the size of the development.[15]

Unfortunately, inclusionary zoning appears potentially to offer little remedy for those areas most in need of affordable housing. In regions with high need, developers can't afford to build enough low-income units without also potentially reducing the incentive for developers to build at all.[16] In addition, inclusionary zoning appears to succeed more in economic redistribution than it does in racial redistribution, for reasons having to do with differential access. Those who line up to take advantage of low-income units are more likely to be connected via social networks to the people who already live in the surrounding area, and those connections tend to be more same-race. The recent real-estate crash makes inclusionary development less effective an option in integrating neighborhoods.

Generate a Parallel Loop

A third and perhaps more promising option is to generate parallel feed-back loops for communities of color. The idea here is to jumpstart pro-cesses—networks of acquaintance and family assistance—with enough resources so that networks and feedback loops create wealth on behalf of those who have been racially excluded.

The key to making a parallel loop strategy work is to provide enough initial resources to make the loops benefit communities of color, whether those resources come from the state or from the private sector. Indeed, resource levels are critical, because social networks that connect people with few resources to each other can actually deepen disadvantage.[17] Resources must be injected into the right networks, in the right places, to get parallel loops up and going. Given that home buying and college attendance are prime ways that white families acquire wealth, policy makers could begin by subsidizing home buying or college attendance for poor black and Latino families, for several generations, to jump-start their wealth accumulation.

The children's trust fund, or baby bonds, to finance such purchases is one such idea. Even before Darity and Hamilton, in the late 1990s legal scholars Bruce Ackerman and Anne Alstott had proposed that everyone who lives in the US for at least eleven years receive, when they came of age (college or age twenty-one), a grant of $80,000, and then smaller annual income grants called "citizen pensions" when they reach the age of sixty-seven. Ackerman and Alstott proposed to fund such a program via wealth taxes on those who presently enjoy economic privilege, and those who can afford to pay back the investment are asked to.[18] A num-ber of US politicians (including Hillary Clinton) have proposed similar sorts of accounts, with far smaller initial contributions and no repay-ment obligations, to be used for college, buying a house, or retirement savings.[19]

Trust funds aimed in particular at buying homes appear to be a par-ticularly good investment. Home equity constitutes about 44 percent of net worth in the US, and is a whopping 60 percent of middle-class wealth in this country.[20] Helping families of color to buy homes creates benefits in other ways—home ownership is related to neighborhoods and public education (neighborhood effects loop) and social networks (network effects loop). Improvements in home-equity based wealth generate improvements in other feedback loops. Of course, to the extent that residential segregation persists, home ownership investment will still give people of color less return on that investment compared to whites.

Unlike income-based assistance, asset-based policies like children's trust funds help to provide poor people of color with what middle-class whites have enjoyed for years—a head start on accumulating wealth. As detailed in Chapter 2, historically government provided middle-class whites with help in buying suburban homes, via FHA and VA home loans, and excluded people of color from participating in such loan programs.

Generating parallel niche networks also offers a promising possibility. Economist James Rauch has suggested that minority retailers make use of independent buying companies that match retailers with vendors, other retailers, and customers, all with an eye toward developing a niche market for minority consumers.[21] Rauch's buying organization would provide the "who you know" in a network—the connections to key vendors and other retailers that are the key to successful retail business.[22] Although the organizational connections cannot fully provide what informal ties provide, buying organizations can supplement networks with fewer resources.

The notion of separate economies for people of color is one that finds support in the phenomenon of ethnic economies, in markets for particular kinds of goods. In these economies, people rely on ethnic ties with one another to create trusting business relationships and to locate financing. Contemporary ethnic economies include the small grocery stories run by African Americans and then by Koreans on the east coast, and nail salons and the garment industry for South Asians on the West Coast.

But the reach of ethnic economies is limited. This is true for at least two reasons. First, as described earlier, embedded resources in parallel networks are frequently not the same for minority networks as for white networks. Jobs in professional networks tend to be lower-wage. Contacts tend to be lower on the professional hierarchy. For this reason, scholars have described ethnic networks formed among people of color as "the wrong networks," implying that white networks contain superior resources and contacts.[23] Second, minority networks structurally look quite different, in ways that disadvantage people of color. Social networks tend to be smaller and with stronger ties between members. But networks with weak ties permit people to search through a much larger range of search space to find resources and opportunities. Deliberately encouraging ethnic economies is likely to be a limited remedy at best, one that works only so long as communities are segregated racially and resources continue to be scarce.

Critical Mass and Affirmative Action

The toughest feedback loop to dismantle might well be the loop that reproduces the power to choose and the rules of distribution. In this loop, whites benefit because they were the first to populate professions and industries. They were able to choose the criteria for hiring, promotion and firing, and, not surprisingly, chose standards that favored themselves.

One potential way to tackle this problem is by putting a critical mass of people of color in a formerly all-white environment via race-based affirmative action. The idea here is that seed groups will potentially disrupt the feedback loop by modifying selection criteria. Economists have suggested that experimental seeding in cluster groups with a critical mass of people can propagate an alternative standard in a group and trigger big change.[24] If the cluster is the right size, a seed group can jump start a switch to another standard, even if the majority of the group is using another standard.[25] Seed groups could help to change the norms and networks that reproduce inequality.

Ideas about seed groups and critical mass draw on empirical research on the way that people make decisions in groups. Organizational change scholar Rosabeth Moss Kanter has studied the way in which a "skewed group"—a group that comprises 85 percent or more of the workplace—comes to dominate and control the culture of an organization. Say for example that whites make up 85 percent of a firm's employees. Kanter (whose work actually focused on gender) argues that a minority group must come to make up between 15 and 35 percent of the workplace before it can really influence workplace culture.

To help transform the workplace, Kanter recommends cluster or batch hiring. Hiring a big number of people of color creates a critical mass, whose members can form coalitions and begin to change workplace norms.[26] Once politically mobilized, these seed groups can help to change the rules of distribution—the hiring criteria, for example—that reproduce disparity. In Kanter's research, cluster hiring increased the likelihood that women would prioritize the hiring of other women or consider family friendly work policies.

Legal Remedies

What about law? Does legal regulation provide some meaningful avenue for dismantling lock-in? Law could work most simply by increasing the cost of continuing the status quo. With regard to intentional discrimination, antidiscrimination law just makes it economically more expensive to discriminate. Discriminating employers have to pay damages or fines if they refuse to hire on the basis of race.

What if law required people (firms) to dismantle their own feedback loops? Title VIII, which prohibits discrimination in housing, appears potentially to require government to affirmatively intervene in some way.[27] Section 3608 of the Fair Housing Act requires the federal government and its agencies to administer its programs in a manner "affirmatively to further" efforts to desegregation and nondiscrimination. Although this provision is rarely enforced effectively as an empirical matter, courts could potentially use Title VIII to require the government to take some sort of affirmative action to remedy racial gaps in housing markets.

At least one pioneering federal district court has aggressively enforced Title VIII's mandate to eliminate the persistent effects of historical discrimination. In *Thompson v. HUD* (2000), plaintiffs sued on the grounds that the city of Baltimore had refused to develop a regional approach to affordable housing. Plaintiffs pointed out that all of the city's affordable housing was located exclusively in the city's poor and predominantly black neighborhoods. Defendants responded that Baltimore neighborhoods and public housing were segregated not because of state action, but because demographic changes such as white flight had resegregated the racial composition of housing residents.

In a robust reading of Title VIII, Judge Marvin Garbis ruled that the law required the Department of Housing and Urban Development (HUD) to undertake affirmative efforts to dismantle the effects of white flight, even though white flight was not directly connected to state action. Judge Garbis also found that HUD had violated the law when the agency failed to consider a regional approach that would have made housing available for Baltimore residents in wealthier, predominantly white communities outside the city. Accordingly, the judge ordered the city to develop a program that located housing in "communities of opportunity."[28] If HUD or other courts followed Garbis's reading of Title VIII as requiring some affirmative government response to white flight and the persistent segregation of housing markets, housing could become an area for significant progress in dismantling some neighborhood effects feedback loops.

Of course, the law might just as easily constrain remedies for lock-in as support remedies. Recent US Supreme Court decisions appear quite hostile to remedies for persistent discrimination that are targeted by race rather than class. In particular, courts have demonstrated their ability to find that race-conscious remedies constitute reverse discrimination against whites.

In *City of Richmond v. J.A. Croson Co.* (1989), the Court struck down a race-conscious remedy for persistent segregation in the city's construction labor market. In that case, the city of Richmond had adopted a minority preference in construction, pointing out that black-owned

construction businesses had less experience largely because blacks historically had been excluded by labor unions and small-business lenders.[29] The Court rejected this argument, finding that societal discrimination was too diffuse to remedy. In the Court's view, eliminating the
persistent effects of societal discrimination would therefore be an end-
less task:

> To accept Richmond's claim that past societal discrimination alone can
> serve as the basis for rigid racial preferences would be to open the door
> to competing claims for "remedial relief" for every disadvantaged group.
> The dream of a Nation of equal citizens in a society where race is irrel-
> evant to personal opportunity and achievement would be lost in a mosaic
> of shifting preferences based on inherently un-measurable claims of past
> wrongs.[30]

In effect, the Court held that remedying widespread societal discrimination was just too big a task for government to take on, at least if it were
going to use race-conscious remedies.[31]

The Court has repeatedly mentioned this fear in subsequent decisions. Although the Court affirmed a limited form of race-conscious
affirmative action in *Grutter v. Bollinger* (2003), it simultaneously struck
down a more targeted form in the same decision, and likewise struck
down race-conscious admissions programs in high school in *Parents
Involved v. Seattle Schools* (2007).[32] In all of those decisions, the Court
noted its fear that continued use of race in policymaking to remedy
persistent inequality would reinforce the very classification it sought to
eliminate. Given the current composition of the Court, race-conscious
legal remedies of any kind might be off the table, at least for the moment.

Conclusion

The preceding chapter does not purport to provide a handbook for policy makers to prescribe ways to dismantle feedback loops or to unlock lock-in. Rather, it points to some very practical implications from the lock-in model that policy makers will have to take into account.

First, time matters. The lock-in process is a dynamic one, and in the case of racial disparity, time makes the problem worse. Where many policy makers assume that the racial gap will eventually narrow, given Becker's arguments about the costliness of discrimination, the lock-in model assumes that time will actually make things worse, as advantage and disadvantage become further entrenched.

Second, the end of discrimination on the basis of race necessarily requires more than the end of intentional discrimination. In the Court's recent decision in *Parents Involved vs. Seattle School District No. 1* (2007), Justice Roberts famously declared that the way to stop discriminating on the basis of race was to stop discriminating on the basis of race. The lock-in model demonstrates why Roberts is wrong—facially race-neutral processes like property taxes and job referral networks reproduce the discrimination of the Jim Crow and slavery eras. Moreover, this book suggests that persistent racial gaps in education, jobs, housing, and wealth are at present as significant or more significant a problem than intentional discrimination.

Third and finally, the concept of critical mass complicates our predictions about what might remedy persistent inequality. Recall from the discussion about tipping points and Polya urns that the dynamics of self-reinforcement frequently involve some dramatic phase transition when the dynamic system hits a critical tipping point. In the urn example, at some key tipping point the variation in the number of colored balls settled down and became locked in.

This concept of tipping point and critical mass has significant implications for remedy as well as cause. For example, a children's trust fund might be completely ineffective until the amount in the fund is large enough to make college a real possibility, or to put a down payment on a house. Short of that number, the children's trust fund isn't really likely to do much work. Once the trust fund hits that critical number—whether it be $80,000 or some other amount—change might begin.

In many conversations about public education, conservative commentators and politicians have argued that money won't solve the problem. These commentators usually cite to the fact that some school districts are enjoying a much higher per capita spending level than other districts, with no appreciable difference in performance.

But if the system exhibits increasing returns or network effects, policy makers might in fact have to throw a lot more money at the problem before the money triggers real change. We understand this intuitively when it comes to physical systems. When heating water, adding more heat might make no appreciable difference for a long period of time until the water hits a critical temperature and then begins to boil. In the same way, critical thresholds might affect the points of change when it comes to persistent racial gaps. Calculating those critical points constitutes an important agenda for scholars of racial inequality to carry forward from here.

Sacramento's Subprime Mortgage Market

Legal scholars Lani Guinier and Gerald Torres have argued that we ought to address racial inequality because racial disparities highlight issues of inequality that affect everyone, rich or poor, black or white. Like the canaries that alerted miners to the poisonous atmosphere in a mine accumulating gas, the problems we have discussed in the preceding chapters are problems that affect all of society, not just people of color. In this networked age, persistent structural inequality can make the entire globe vulnerable.

The subprime mortgage crisis illustrates this point only too well. Even as this chapter is being written, the US economy is in the throes of the most dramatic financial crisis since the Great Depression in the 1930s. In the space of one short week in September of 2008, credit markets disintegrated, several major banks failed, and the stock market lost thousands of points. In the wake of that collapse, Congress passed a trillion dollar bailout package and policy makers partially nationalized US banks. All US residents—not just communities of color—were hard hit, though minorities were hit harder than whites. Global markets have taken a beating as well, and several countries are on the verge of bankruptcy.

The story of global economic collapse contains within it a much smaller and less well-known story: a story of lock-in that involves subprime lending in particular urban communities in the American Southwest, among other places. In this story, historical discrimination created concentrated pockets of people of color with few assets and low income, in cities like Sacramento, Las Vegas, Fort Myers, and Phoenix. The segregated pockets of low-income and low-wealth minority residents created ready-made markets for the kind of high-risk lending that would come to undo the market for everyone.

Sociologist Jesus Hernandez narrates this story of lock-in and its connection to the economic crash in the city of Sacramento.[1] In Sacramento's early history, whites engaged in cartel conduct to give whites monopoly access to the city's best property. As was true for many cities, Sacramento had a long and sordid history of racial segregation in residential housing markets. As early as 1918, the city's white real estate brokers and homeowners worked together to keep blacks out of white Sacramento neighborhoods. Developers of suburban tracts in the Sacramento region worked together with homeowners to exclude minority residents from elite white enclaves. Informal social norms and then, later, federal housing program requirements created pressure on homeowners to adopt racially restrictive covenants to exclude as a condition for getting financing or federal loan approval. Working collectively, white homeowners' associations and developers drafted racially restrictive covenants for white neighborhoods and signed residents up.

Such cartel conduct divided up the city into a dual market. Because areas like the West End of Sacramento were redlined and unable to get financing for new housing purchases or property improvements, these areas deteriorated. The property values in the area plummeted by 30 percent, despite an overall increase in property values for Sacramento of 46 percent. By 1950, 87 percent of the city's Mexican residents, 75 percent of Asians, and 60 percent of black residents lived in the city's West End, with aging housing stock and a declining business presence.

Hernandez documents the timeline of the mortgage crisis from its early history. Beginning in 1950, greater numbers of blacks and Mexicans migrated into Sacramento. Blacks came primarily because of the military, and Mexicans came in connection with the Bracero program. In response, white real estate professionals, developers, and homeowners dramatically stepped up their exclusionary efforts. Realtors in the city organized with others to pass Proposition 14, a statewide referendum that voided those state fair housing laws that prohibited racial discrimination in real estate sales and rentals.

In the second act of the story, in the 1950s and '60s, urban renewal programs relocated minority neighborhoods from the West End to much poorer white neighborhoods that had not adopted restrictive covenants. These poor neighborhoods were subject to even more rampant redlining than the West End had been. At the same time, those neighborhoods with restrictive covenants remained white and experienced much less turnover. The East Sacramento, Land Park, and Curtis Park neighborhoods were almost homogenously white, even after racial covenants were outlawed.

By the 1970s, neighborhood boundaries had become entrenched, and mortgage redlining against neighborhoods of color had become standard practice. Capital flowed freely to white neighborhoods but slowed to a trickle to neighborhoods with people of color. At the beginning of the 1980s, Sacramento was geographically divided by both race and class. And the concentrated pockets of low-income families of color created ready-made markets for subprime lenders, as they did in cities across the country.

The map of subprime lending in Sacramento is essentially identical to the 1980s map of racial and class segregation. Subprime lending as a financial service faced several hurdles at the outset. First, the lenders had to convince Congress to deregulate high-risk lending for high-risk buyers. In 1980, Congress enacted legislation to get rid of usury restrictions on mortgage rates, allowing lenders to charge higher rates of interest to borrowers who presumably had higher credit risk. In other legislation passed in 1982, Congress permitted lenders to use variable or adjustable interest rates and balloon payments on loans to higher-risk borrowers.

As Hernandez notes, tax legislation enacted in 1996 eliminated the tax deduction on consumer credit interest. This change made mortgage debt more attractive than consumer debt. The change also permitted the sale of mortgage-backed securities and allowed the terms to vary according to the risk of the loans. These options created a new pool of secondary investors, who bought mortgage-backed securities for subprime loans. An increase in the Federal Reserve Board's lending rate made subprimes even more attractive. Nationwide, subprime loans increased by 25 percent between 1994 and 2003. Much of the subprime lending markets focused on low-income families of color.

In Sacramento, as in other cities, low-income lending targeted the very same poor and working-class minority neighborhoods that had been the victims of mortgage redlining in the 1970s. Indeed, as Hernandez points out, the census tracts of Sacramento that were redlined prior to 1970 were the very same census tracts most affected by subprime lending. Tracts that were redlined and were not subject to restrictive covenants show very high rates of subprime lending.

Not coincidentally in the wake of the crash, these areas now show a high rate of FHA loan denials and of foreclosure. South Sacramento neighborhoods currently have some of the highest foreclosure rates in the entire country. These neighborhoods were those redlined in the 1970s, those that were the target of subprime lending in the '90s, and those that were consequently very vulnerable to economic shock in 2008.

The subprime crisis has now generated a self-reinforcing feedback loop that further locks in historical disadvantage for communities of color. Paradoxically, at its outset, subprime lending actually looked like a way for those previously excluded communities to create wealth by buying a house. But as the real estate market declined because of over-building, communities of color became disproportionately vulnerable to subprime lending. Owing to their previous disadvantage, black and Latino residents in Sacramento were much more likely to be saddled with mortgage rates that reset after an initial period to much higher rates.[2]

Sacramento's experience reflects the picture in cities across the country, where blacks and Latinos were far more likely than whites to have had subprime loans. To be sure, people of color have been more likely to receive subprime loans even after controlling for creditworthiness, suggesting that such loans were racially targeted. But even in the absence of intentional targeting, structural conditions explain why these Sacramento neighborhoods were vulnerable to such lending, and then to economic collapse.

The mortgage crisis is important for another reason. It demonstrates the inefficiency of persistent inequality. More specifically, the mortgage crisis illuminates the way in which the welfare of wealthy whites is now tied via financial networks to the welfare of poor and working-class people of color, in an ecological web of connections. Financial products like mortgage-backed securities connect the wealth of poor and working-class people of color to the wealth of the richer whites. As a result, when an economic shock pushed people of color further into disadvantage, the country's credit markets, and indeed global credit markets, were pushed into crisis as well, for rich as well as poor.

Given that the subprime crisis affected wealthy whites' economic well-being, policy makers are now far more willing to consider government intervention to correct for market failure. Even conservative commentators have conceded that government relief (affirmative action?) was a necessary step to put the country's economic future back on track. But back when subprime foreclosures affected communities of color exclusively, those same policy makers and legislators opposed government intervention. Only now, it seems, have they come to recognize the interdependencies of locked-in inequality.

Even neoclassical economics will concede that a market that concentrates advantage for some by displacing costs on others is an inefficient market. But the notion of monopoly is not just a symbol of inefficiency, it is also, in the American consciousness, a symbol of unfairness. The great robber barons of the Gilded Age accumulated wealth with no limit because they were playing by unfair rules. In modern notions of antitrust, anyone familiar with the government's case against Microsoft generally understands the notion of monopoly and what makes it unfair.

The lock-in model explains why historical monopoly reproduces itself generation after generation, long after bad behavior has stopped. Perhaps the lock-in model is most useful in this regard, in that it connects current disparity with historical misconduct. Understanding the principles of lock-in, we can see the unfairness of historical advantage as something that affects contemporary conditions.

In the context of monopoly, people also understand quite quickly the need for significant government intervention. In the absence of restructuring, the everyday processes that we take for granted—referring our friends for a job, choosing a neighborhood with well-financed public schools, giving our children money for college tuition—will continue to reproduce racial inequality. The lock-in story of inequality accomplishes a great deal if it persuades us that we ought to move quickly toward the more inclusionary path, before locked-in racial disparities become a permanent and unchanging part of the American landscape.

NOTES

NOTES TO THE INTRODUCTION

1. Paul Krugman, Op-Ed., *It's a Different Country*, New York Times, June 9, 2008.

2. John McWhorter, Op-Ed., *It's Official: America is 'Post-Racial' in the Age of Obama*, The Grio, January 14, 2010.

3. Thomas M. Shapiro et al., *The Racial Wealth Gap Increases Fourfold*, Inst. on Assets & Soc. Pol'y, (May 2010). Importantly, this study did not take into account home equity, because equity cannot be drawn out and replaced; given the disparate impact of the foreclosure crisis on families of color, it's likely the gap would be much larger if home equity had been factored in.

4. Maria Cancian & Sheldon Danzinger, Changing Poverty, Changing Policies (2009).

5. Stuart Gabriel & Stuart Rosenthal, *Homeownership in the 1980s and 1990s: Aggregate Trends and Racial Gaps*, 57 J. Urb. Econ. 101, 103 (2005).

6. Rakesh Kochhar et al., *Wealth Gaps Rise to Record Highs Between Whites, Blacks and Hispanics*, Pew Res. Ctr., 31 (July 26, 2011).

7. *Id.* at 29–30.

8. Sylvia A. Allegretto, *The State of Working America's Wealth, 2011: Through Volatility and Turmoil, the Gap Widens*, Econ. Policy Inst., 10 (Briefing Paper No. 292), (Mar. 23, 2011) (based on a 2010 unpublished analysis of Survey of Consumer Finances by Edward Wolff).

9. *Id.* at 9.

10. Carolyn J. Hill & Harry Holzer, *Labor Market Experiences and Transition to Adulthood, in* The Price of Independence: The Economics of Early Adulthood 141–69 (Sheldon Danziger & Cecilia Elena Rouse eds., 2007).

11. *One in 100: Behind Bars in America 2008*, Pew Res. Ctr. on the States 3 (2008).

12. *Id.* at 6.

13. Christopher Wildeman & Bruce Western, *Incarceration in Fragile Families*, 20 Future Child 157 (Fall 2010).

14. Becky Pettit & Bruce Western, *Mass Imprisonment and the Life Course: Race and Class Inequality in U.S. Incarceration*, 69 Am. Sociol. Rev. 151 (2004).

15. Marian MacDorman & T. J. Mathews, *Understanding Racial and Ethnic Disparities in U.S. Infant Mortality Rates*, NCHS Data Brief No. 74, 1 (US Dep't of Health & Hum. Serv.) (Sept. 2011).

16. *See* W. Brian Arthur, *Competing Technologies, Increasing Returns, and Lock-In by Historical Events,* 99 Econ. J. 116 (1989).

17. United States v. Microsoft Corp., 159 F.R.D. 318 (D.C. Cir. 1995).

18. *Id.* Judge Stanley Sporkin's Memorandum opinion in *US v. Microsoft* was issued on Feb. 14, 1995. Judge Sporkin refused to approve the US Government's proposed judgment in the case, finding that it did not sufficiently restore the competition to the operating systems market.

19. For an extensive discussion of both the allegations against Microsoft and the arguments about increasing returns, *see* Memorandum of Amici Curiae in Opposition to Proposed Final Judgment, *United States v. Microsoft Corp.*, 159 F.R.D. 318 (D.C. Cir. 1995) (No. 94-1564).

20. For a more detailed analysis, *see* Max Schanzenbach, *Network Effects and Antitrust Law: Predation, Affirmative Defenses, and the Case of US v. Microsoft*, 2002 Stan. Tech. L. Rev. 4 (2002).

NOTES TO CHAPTER 1

1. Richard J. Herrnstein & Charles Murray, The Bell Curve (1994).

2. Stephen Jay Gould, The Mismeasure of Man (1996).

3. Claude Steele & Joshua Aronson, *Stereotype Threat and the Intellectual Test Performance of African Americans*, 69 J. Personality & Soc. Psych. 797 (1995).

4. Christopher Winship & Sanders Korenman, *A Reanalysis of the Bell Curve: Intelligence, Family Background and Schooling, in* Meritocracy and Economic Inequality (2000); Robert Hauser & Min Hsiang Huang, *Verbal Ability and Socio-economic Success: A Trend Analysis*, 26 Soc. Sci. Res. 331 (1997); James Heckman, *Lessons From the Bell Curve*, 103 J. Pol. Econ. 1091 (1995). For a collection of the main critical arguments, *see* Claude S. Fischer et al., Inequality by Design: Cracking the Bell Curve Myth (1996).

5. Joe L. Kincheloe et al., Measured Lies: The Bell Curve Examined (1996); Steven Fraser, The Bell Curve Wars: Race, Intelligence, and the Future of America (1995); Bob Herbert, Op-Ed., *In America; Throwing a Curve*, New York Times, Oct. 26, 1994.

6. Gary Becker, The Economics of Discrimination (2d ed. 1957).

7. *Id.*

8. *Id.*

9. Kenneth J. Arrow, *The Theory of Discrimination, in* Discrimination in Labor Markets (Orley Ashenfelter and Albert Rees eds., 1973); Edmund Phelps, *The Statistical Theory of Racism and Sexism*, 62 Am. Econ. Rev. 659 (1972).

10. Arrow, *The Theory of Discrimination*.

11. The standard citation to these ideas is Joan Robinson, The Economics of Imperfect Competition (1934). For more recent treatments, *see* Francine D. Blau et al., The Economics of Women, Men and Work (1998).

12. *See, e.g.*, Samuel George Morton, Crania Americana: Or, A Comparative View of the Skulls of Various Aboriginal Nations of North and South America (1839).

13. Gould, The Mismeasure of Man.

14. Lawrence D. Bobo, *Racial Attitudes and Relations at the Close of the Twentieth Century, in* America Becoming: Racial Trends and Their Consequences 265, 295 (Neil J. Smelser et al. eds., 2001).

15. *See M.* Bertrand & S. Mullainathan, *Are Emily and Greg More Employable than Lakisha and Jamal? A Field Experiment on Labor Market Discrimination*, 94 Am. Econ. Rev. 991 (2004).

16. Margery Austin Turner et al., *Discrimination in Metropolitan Housing Markets: National Results from Phase 1 of HDS 2000*, Urb. Inst. 6–16 (2002).

17. William A. Darity & Samuel L. Myers, Persistent Disparity: Race and Economic Inequality in the United States since 1945 (1998).

18. Lincoln Quillian, *New Approaches to Understanding Racial Prejudice and Discrimination*, 32 Ann. Rev. Sociol. 299 (2006) (reviewing work by Bobo, Bonilla-Silva and others on "kinder and gentler" antiblack attitudes).

19. For a detailed review of the implicit bias research, *see* C.T. Smith & Brian A. Nosek, *Implicit Association Test in* I. B. Weiner and W. E. Craighead, Corsini's Encyclopedia of Psychology 803–04 (4th ed. 2010).

20. Scott Ottaway et al., *Implicit Attitudes and Racism: Effects of Word Familiarity and Frequency on the Implicit Association Test*, 19 Soc. Cog. 97 (2001).

21. Phillip E. Tetlock & Gregory Mitchell, *Implicit Bias and Accountability Systems: What Must Organizations Do to Prevent Discrimination?*, 29 Res. Org. Behav. 3 (2009).

22. *See* for example, Hart Blanton et al., *Strong Claims and Weak Evidence: Reassessing the Predictive Validity of the IAT*, 94 J. Appl. Psych. 567 (2009).

23. Jens Agerstrom & Dan-Olof Rooth, *Implicit Prejudice and Ethnic Minorities: Arab-Muslims in Sweden*, 30 Int'l J. Manpower 43 (2009).

24. Oscar Lewis, The Culture of Poverty (1966).

25. Daniel P. Moynihan, The Negro Family: The Case for National Action (1965).

26. *See* Carol B. Stack, All Our Kin: Strategies For Survival in a Black Community (1974); Eleanor Burke Leacock, The Culture of Poverty: A Critique (1971); Charles A. Valentine, Culture and Poverty: Critique and Counter-Proposals (1968). Michael Harrington defended Lewis and Moynihan in The New American Poverty (1984).

27. For example, Carol Stack provided an alternative view of kinship networks that actually stabilized many families. For a general discussion of the critiques of the report, *see* William Julius Wilson, More Than Just Race: Being Black and Poor in

the Inner City (2009); Michael B. Katz, The Undeserving Poor: From the War on Poverty to the War on Welfare (1989).

28. Stephan Thernstrom & Abigail Thernstrom, No Excuses: Closing the Racial Gap in Learning 112 (2003).

29. Thomas Sowell, Ethnic America: A History (1981).

30. Wilson, More Than Just Race: Being Black and Poor in the Inner City.

31. Glenn Loury, *A Dynamic Theory of Racial Income Differences, in* Women, Minorities and Employment Discrimination (Phyllis A. Wallace & Annette M. LaMond eds., 1977).

32. *Id.* Likewise, Shelly Lundberg and Richard Startz, argued that when discrimination makes it more difficult for a group to acquire human capital, this difficulty gets passed down to the next generation via group effects. Shelly Lundberg & Richard Startz, *On the Persistence of Racial Inequality*, 16 J. Labor Econ. 292 (1998).

NOTES TO CHAPTER 2

1. The story of the Memphis hate strike is well-chronicled in Erik Arnesen's account of racial exclusion on the railroad. *See* Erik Arnesen, Brotherhoods of Color: Black Railroad Workers and the Struggle for Equality 65–69 (2001).

2. *Id.* at 66, 69–70.

3. The success of the hate strike in Memphis signaled a major shift for the railroad industry. Nationwide, after this strike, white unions began to regularly demand racially restrictive contractual clauses, and most railroad union contracts began to carry them. *Id.* at 70–73, 75.

4. *Id.* at 67–68.

5. *Id.* at 68–69.

6. *Id.*

7. Becker, The Economics of Discrimination.

8. *See* Arnesen, Brotherhoods of Color: Black Railroad Workers and the Struggle for Equality.

9. *See* W. Brian Arthur, Increasing Returns and Path Dependence in the Economy (1994).

10. Becker, The Economics of Discrimination, at 43–45; *see also* Joseph Stiglitz, Economics 410 (1993). Becker actually hypothesized that market monopolies as a species of market failure would permit individuals to indulge in a "taste" for discrimination. Becker, The Economics of Discrimination, 46–47.

11. *See* 3 The New Palgrave: A Dictionary of Economics 343 (John Eatwell et al. eds., 1987).

12. *See* The New Palgrave Dictionary of Economics and the Law 206–11 (Peter Newman ed., 1998). For a much fuller discussion of cartel definitions, and proof of the existence of cartels under US and European Community law, *see* Maurice Guerrin & Georgios Kyriazis, *Cartels: Proof and Procedural Issues*, 16 Fordham Int'l L.J. 266 (1992).

13. George W. Stocking & Myron W. Watkins, Cartels in Action: Case Studies in International Business Diplomacy 5–10 (1946).

14. *Id.*

15. Becker, The Economics of Discrimination, 6–8, 19–38, 58–61.

16. *See* Lester C. Thurow, Generating Inequality: Mechanisms of distribution in the US Economy 118–26 (1975).

17. *See generally* Muzafer Sherif et al., The Robbers Cave Experiment: Intergroup Conflict and Cooperation (Wesleyan rev. ed. 1988).

18. Frank Parkin, Randall Collins, and Robert Murphy draw on and extend the work of Max Weber on closure, to argue that closure is essential to monopolizing scarce resources and opportunities. *See* Robert Murphy, Social Closure: The Theory of Monopolization and Exclusion (1988); Randall Collins, Conflict Sociology: Towards An Explanatory Science (1975); Frank Parkin, *Strategies of Social Closure in Class Formation, in* The Social Analysis of Class Structure (Frank Parkin ed., 1972).

19. Sherif et al., The Robbers Cave Experiment: Intergroup Conflict and Cooperation.

20. Robert Cooter, *Market Affirmative Action*, 31 San Diego L. Rev. 133 (1994).

21. *See* Avinash Dixit & Barry Nalebuff, Thinking Strategically (1991); Thomas C. Schelling, The Strategy of Conflict (1960).

22. For a formal modeling of the defector problem, *see* Peter C. Cramton & Thomas R. Palfrey, *Cartel Enforcement with Uncertainty About Costs*, 31 Int'l Econ. Rev. 17 (1990).

23. Mancur Olson famously has described the free-rider problem at length. *See* Mancur Olson, The Logic of Collective Action: Public Goods and the Theory of Groups 21–36 (1971).

24. For a study of enduring cartels generally, *see* How Cartels Endure and How They Fail: Studies of Industrial Collusion (Peter Z. Grossman ed., 2004).

25. *See* Robert Boyd et al., *The Evolution of Altruistic Punishment,* 100 Proc. Nat'l Acad. Sci. 3531 (2003).

26. *See* Donald Massey & Nancy Denton, American Apartheid: Segregation and the Making of the Underclass 41 (1998) (documenting that a Baltimore segregation ordinance reserved some neighborhoods for blacks and others for whites); Buchanan v. Warley, 245 US 60, 70–75 (1917) (describing the Louisville ordinance, which the Court struck down as unconstitutional).

27. John Hope Franklin, Reconstruction After the Civil War 47–50 (1994).

28. Jennifer Roback, *Southern Labor Law in the Jim Crow Era: Exploitative or Competitive?*, 51 U. Chi. L. Rev. 1161, 1169 (1984).

29. *Gandolfo v. Hartman,* 49 F. 181 (C.C.S.D. Cal. 1892), records the case of a restrictive covenant that prohibited the sale of property to Chinese residents in California. *Clifton v. Puente*, 218 S.W. 2d 272 (Texas Civ. App. 1949), discusses a restrictive covenant that prohibited sale to persons of "Mexican descent" in Texas. Restrictive covenants prohibiting sale to blacks were numerous, and were only invalidated in 1948, in the case of *Shelley v. Kraemer*, 334 US 1 (1948).

30. *See Kraemer*, 334 US 1 (1948).

31. Richard Brooks has argued that even after restrictive covenants were outlawed in *Shelly v. Kraemer*, restrictive covenants continued to produce residential segregation by signaling the racial exclusivity of white communities and by functioning as an informal social norm enforced via social sanctions and incentives. Richard R.W. Brooks, *Covenants and Conventions*, (Northwestern Law & Econ. Res. Paper No. 02-8, Sept. 2002).

32. Rose Helper, Racial Policies and Practices of Real Estate Brokers 116–17, 136 (1969).

33. Sheldon Stryker & Richard T. Serpe, *Identity Salience and Psychological Centrality: Equivalent, Overlapping or Complementary Concepts?*, 57 Soc. Psych. Q. 16 (1994). The distinction between external and internal incentives is not sharp, and indeed the two categories are linked. According to social psychologists, people often internalize attitudes and beliefs when they are externally rewarded for doing so (or punished for not doing so). People are also more likely to internalize a group norm or role if doing so will reduce the amount of time the person spends deciding how to act during moments of uncertainty. Edward L. Deci, & Richard M. Ryan, Intrinsic Motivation and Self-Determination in Human Behavior 132–33 (1985); J. Richard Hackman & Charles G. Morris, *Group Tasks, Group Interaction Process, and Group Performance Effectiveness: A Review and Proposed Integration, in* Advances in Experimental Social Psychology (L. Berkowitz ed., 1998).

34. Sheldon Stryker has laid out many of these key concepts in his book Symbolic Interactionism: A Social Structural Version (1980). For an overview of identity theory, *see* Sheldon Stryker & Peter Burke, *The Past, Present and Future of an Identity Theory*, 63 Soc. Psych. Q. 284 (2000).

35. This example is considered in far more detail in Chapter 3.

36. *See* the more detailed discussion in Chapter 3.

37. *See* Mary R. Jackman & Robert W. Jackman, *Racial Inequalities in Home Ownership*, 58 Soc. Forces 1221, 1227–30 (1980) (documenting property value differences between black and white homes).

38. *See* Gary Becker, The Economics of Discrimination, 19–38.

39. *See* Gavin Wright, Old South, New South (1986); Robert Margo, *The Competitive Dynamics of Racial Exclusion: Employment Segregation in the South, 1900 to 1950, in* Race and Schooling in the South, 1880–1950: An Economic History (1990).

40. *See* Kenneth T. Jackson, *Race, Ethnicity and Real Estate Appraisal: The Home Owners' Loan Corporation and the Federal Housing Administration*, 6 J. Urb. His. 419 (1980).

41. Gareth Davies & Martha Derthick, *Race and Social Welfare Policy: The Social Security Act of 1935*, 112 Pol. Sci. Q. 217 (1997); Marc Linder, *Farm Workers and the Fair Labor Standards Act*, 65 Tex. L. Rev. 1335, 1336 (1987).

42. *See* Camille Guerin-Gonzales, Mexican American Workers and American Dreams: Immigration, Repatriation, and California Farm Labor, 1900–1939, at 63–69 (1994); Gilbert G. Gonzales, Labor and Community: Mexican Citrus

Worker Villages in a Southern California County, 1900–1950, at 188 (1994). *See also* Becker, The Economics of Discrimination, 73.

43. Leon F. Litwack, North of Slavery: The Negro in the Free States, 1790–1860, at 114 (1961). *See* Joseph M. Kousser, The Shaping of Southern Politics: Suffrage Restriction and the Establishment of the One-Party South, 1880–1910 (1974). Sean D. Cashman, African-Americans and the Quest for Civil Rights, 1900–1990, at 132–34 (1992). For a discussion on how the homeowners association in Chicago used inexplicit ways to exclude blacks from their neighborhoods, *see* Zorita Mikva, The Neighborhood Improvement Association: A Counter-force to the Expansion of Chicago's Negro Population (June 1951) (unpublished MA dissertation, Univ. of Chicago).

NOTES TO CHAPTER 3

1. *See* Kraemer, 334 US at 4–7, 18–20 (describing racially restrictive covenants). *See also* Massey & Denton, American Apartheid, 36–37.

2. Burke v. Kleiman, 277 Ill. App. 519, 523 (1934)

3. Wendy Plotkin, *"Hemmed In": The Struggle Against Racial Restrictive Covenants and Deed Restrictions in Post-WWII Chicago*, 94 J. Ill. St. Hist. Soc'y. 39 (2001). *See also* Lorraine Hansberry, To Be Young, Gifted, and Black (1970).

4. Hansberry, To Be Young, Gifted, and Black, 51.

5. Hansberry v. Lee, 311 US 32 (1940).

6. *See* Chapter 3 and the discussion about homeowners' associations and political parties.

7. *See* Leon Litwack, North of Slavery: The Negro in the Free States 6, 47 (1965).

8. *Id.* at 75–77 (voting); 114–20 (education); 156–57 (labor market).

9. *Id.* at 162–65.

10. *Id.* at 166–67.

11. *Id.* at 164–67.

12. Massey & Denton, American Apartheid, 20. The segregation index ranges from 0, which reflects a thoroughly mixed population, to 1, which reflects a completely segregated population. An index of .50 means that 50 percent of blacks would have had to move to a neighborhood where the black percentage is lower to shift the city toward evenness. *Id.* According to Stanley Lieberson, in 1890, on the average, blacks lived in Chicago neighborhoods that were 8 percent black. Stanley Lieberson, A Piece of the Pie: Blacks and White Immigrants Since 1880, at 266, 288 (1980).

13. For a good overview of the contours of black migration to the North, *see* Massey & Denton, American Apartheid, *supra* note 78; Thomas Lee Philpott, The Slum and The Ghetto: Immigrants, Blacks, and Reformers in Chicago, 1880–1930 (2d ed. 1991).

14. Alan Spear, Black Chicago: The Making of A Negro Ghetto 1890–1920, at 11 (1967).

15. Massey & Denton, American Apartheid, 29. In 1850, 77 percent of Chicago residents were of foreign origin, and over 400,000 had arrived during the wave of immigration that occurred during 1880. Philpott, The Slum and the Ghetto, 117.

16. Philpott, The Slum and the Ghetto, 147.

17. Massey & Denton, American Apartheid, 20. *See also* Philpott, Slum and the Ghetto, 133; Spear, Black Chicago, 20–21.

18. Zorita Mikva, The Neighborhood Improvement Association: A Counter-force to the Expansion of Chicago's Negro Population.

19. Rose Helper, Racial Policies and Practices of Real Estate Brokers, 4.

20. Philpott, The Slum and the Ghetto, 185.

21. *Id.* at 190–92.

22. Michael Jones-Correa, *The Origins and Diffusion of Racial Restrictive Covenants*, 115 Pol. Sci. Q. 541, 564–66 (Winter 2000–2001).

23. *See id.* Chicago community leader Nathan MacChesney drafted the code provision. Philpott, The Slum and the Ghetto, 190.

24. Michael Jones-Correa, *The Origins and Diffusion of Racial Restrictive Covenants*, 564–65.

25. Massey & Denton, American Apartheid, 51–52.

26. *Id.* at 54.

27. *See id.*

28. Philpott, Slum and the Ghetto, 154–55.

29. Massey & Denton, American Apartheid, 34–35.

30. Philpott, Slum and the Ghetto, 154–55.

31. Brooks, *Covenants and Conventions*, 11–12.

32. Philpott, The Slum and the Ghetto, 186–95.

33. *Id.* at 44–63 (describing structure and size of associations, their coalitions with other associations within political boundaries, their connection with larger regional federations).

34. *Id.* at 101–02, note 3. One homeowner was approached by a realty company to ask that he put his house for sale through their company, *before* he had put his home up. He suspected that the firm had learned of the potential sale through the Field Secretary of his regional association. *Id.* at 84.

35. *Id.* at 101.

36. *Id.* at 103–04.

37. *Id.* at 136.

38. Helper, Racial Policies and Practices of Real Estate Brokers, 116–17.

39. *Id.* at 119.

40. *Id. See also* Dmitri Mehlhorn, *A Requiem for Blockbusting: Lace, Economics and Race-Based Real Estate Speculation*, 67 Fordham L. Rev. 1145 (1998).

41. Helper, Racial Policies and Practices of Real Estate Brokers.

42. Kousser, The Shaping of Southern Politics, 6–8.

43. C. Vann Woodward, Origins of the New South 222, 229 (Wendell Holmes Stephenson & E. Merton Coulter eds., 1995); Kousser, The Shaping of Southern Politics, 16–17.

44. V.O. Key, Jr., Southern Politics in State and Nation (1977). Similarly, Michael Perman has suggested that the conservative black-belt Democrats did not lead the movement in every state—in some states, like South Carolina and Mississippi, independent dissenters spearheaded the push for disfranchisement, and black-belt Democrats opposed the move or were slow to join it. Michael Perman, Struggle for Mastery, Disfranchisement in the South 1888–1908, at 2–8, 321–24 (2001).

45. Ray Marshall, Industrialization and Race Relations in the Southern United States, in Industrialization and Race Relations 61 (1965). See also Harold M. Baron, The Demand for Black Labor: Historical Notes on the Political Economy of Racism, 5 Radical Am. 9 (1971) (arguing that nonslaveholders had no power to pass laws to restrict slave labor practices).

46. John Hope Franklin, From Slavery to Freedom 283 (8th ed. 2000); C. Vann Woodward, The Strange Career of Jim Crow 77 (1955).

47. John Hope Franklin, From Slavery to Freedom, 284; Vann Woodward, Origins of the New South, 192–93. The Southern Alliance joined with the Western Farmer's Alliance to form the National Farmers' Alliance, and much like the southerners, the national organization united small farmland owners with hired hands to promote radical agrarian interests. Franklin, From Slavery to Freedom, 284; Vann Woodward, Origins of the New South, 193, 246. A range of other economic programs produced independent movements as well. Morgan Kousser chronicles the rise of the Readjusters in Virginia, the Greenbacks in a number of southern states, the antiprohibitionists in North Carolina, those opposed to land giveaways in Florida, and the Agricultural Wheel in Arkansas (which eventually became part of the Farmers' Alliance). Kousser, The Shaping of Southern Politics, 25. See also Vann Woodward, The Strange Career of Jim Crow, 60.

48. Vann Woodward, Origins of the New South, 236, 254–56; Vann Woodward, Strange Career of Jim Crow, 60.

49. Franklin, From Slavery to Freedom, 281; Vann Woodward, Origins of the New South, 251, 255.

50. Kousser, The Shaping of Southern Politics, 196. To be sure, Texas was the least "Southern" of the southern states, and had internalized far less of the fixed racial attitude and the hierarchical elitist power structure, having had a relatively shorter experience with slavery. But competition among whites was, as a result, far more open and a Democratic victory less assured than in other states. White Democrats struggled repeatedly against a coalition of poor whites and blacks (and in some cases Mexicans) for power and office, and the third-party movement was stronger in Texas than anywhere else in the South. Id. at 97.

51. Id.

52. For a detailed review of the history of the white primary, *see* Darlene Clark Hine, *Black Victory: The Rise and Fall of the White Primary in Texas* (2003).

53. Competition for black votes first became a real issue during the election of 1892, and some black officials were voted in during this election. *Id.* at 198.

54. *Nixon v. Herndon*, 273 US 536 (1927).

55. In *Nixon v. Condon*, 286 US 73 (1932), the Court struck down a restriction limiting membership to whites in this second round, again on Fourteenth Amendment grounds. Determined to get past the Supreme Court's objections, the Democratic State Convention (a much larger group with far more direct participation than the Executive Committee) adopted a resolution restricting membership on the basis of race. For an extended discussion of these historical events, *see* Hine, *Black Victory: The Rise and Fall of the White Primary in Texas*.

56. In *Grovey v. Townsend*, 295 US 25 (1935), the Supreme Court approved the convention's restrictions, finding on the basis of the party's "private" status that Texas had not taken any state action to violate the Fourteenth Amendment. A few years later, however, in *Smith v. Allwright*, 321 US 649 (1944), the Court reversed itself, finding that state law so extensively pervaded the party's participation in elections that the Convention constituted illegal state action.

57. Hine, *Black Victory: The Rise and Fall of the White Primary in Texas*.

58. *Id.* at 245–46.

59. *Id.* at 78.

60. *Id.* at 81.

61. *Id.* at 245–46.

62. *Id.* at 84.

63. *Terry v. Adams*, 345 US 461 (1953).

64. Samuel Issacharoff & Richard H. Pildes, *Politics as Markets: Partisan Lockups of the Democratic Process*, 50 Stan. L. Rev. 643 (1998).

65. *Id.* at 663.

NOTES TO CHAPTER 4

1. Shelly J. Lundberg & Richard Startz, *Inequality and Race: Models and Policy*, in Meritocracy and Economic Inequality (Kenneth Arrow et al. eds., 2000).

2. For a highly readable introduction to complex systems theory, including the narrative of the genre's evolution, *see* M. Mitchell Waldrop, Complexity: The Emerging Science at the Edge of Order and Chaos (1993). For a more technical discussion of the principles of complex systems, *see* Robert Axelrod & Michael D. Cohen, Harnessing Complexity: Organizational Implications of a Scientific Frontier (2001). For an introduction somewhere in the middle, *see* W. Brian Arthur, *Why Do Things Become More Complex?*, Sci. Am. 144 (May 1993).

3. In physical systems, such points are often referred to as phase transitions. For example, when water moves from frozen form to fluid, the phase transition takes place within the context of a small increase in temperature. Other complex

systems display tipping points, critical thresholds and other phenomena in which small differences create large changes. A small outbreak of an infectious disease suddenly becomes an epidemic. The centuries-old practice of foot binding disappears over thirty years. For a very readable description of this feature of complex systems, *see* Malcolm Gladwell, The Tipping Point: How Little Things Can Make a Big Difference (2002).

4. Gunnar Myrdal, Economic Theory and Underdeveloped Regions (1957); Nicholas Kaldor, Cases of the Slow Rate of Economic Growth (1966).

5. W. Brian Arthur, *Increasing Returns and the Two Worlds of Business*, Harv. Bus. Rev. 100 (July–August 1996).

6. For a vigorous defense of Microsoft's conduct, a challenge to the lock-in argument, and an argument that Microsoft's dominance can be traced to a better product, *see* Stanley J. Liebowitz & Steven E. Margolis, Winners, Losers & Microsoft: Competition and Antitrust in High Technology (2001).

7. Microsoft v. United States, No. 94-1564, Mem. Op. and J (D.D.C. 1995).

8. These results hold true in studies that control for income and other factors. *See* Melvin Oliver & Thomas Shapiro, Black Wealth/White Wealth: A New Perspective on Racial Inequality 7 (2006) (reporting 15 percent); Thomas M. Shapiro, The Hidden Cost of Being African American: How Wealth Perpetuates Inequality 47 (2004); Francine D. Blau & John W. Graham, *Black-White Differences in Wealth and Asset Composition*, 105 Q. J. Econ. 321, 321 (1990) (reporting 18 percent).

9. Shapiro, The Hidden Cost of Being African American: How Wealth Perpetuates Inequality, 47.

10. Rakesh Kochhar, *The Wealth of Hispanic Households: 1996 to 2002*, Pew Hispanic Ctr. 2 (Oct. 18, 2004).

11. Rakesh Kochhar et al., *Wealth Gaps Rise to Record Highs Between Whites.*

12. Laurence J. Kotlikoff & Lawrence H. Summers, *The Contribution of Intergenerational Transfers to Total Wealth: A Reply*, 11 (NBER Working Paper No. 1827, 1986) (reviewing evidence accumulated after 1981); *see also* Laurence J. Kotlikoff & Lawrence H. Summers, *The Role of Intergenerational Transfers in Aggregate Capital Accumulation*, 89 J. Pol. Econ. 706, 730 (1981) (intergenerational transfers are the "major element determining wealth accumulation" in the US in 1974, eliminating intergenerational transfers would have reduced wealth by $3 trillion).

13. *See* Oliver & Shapiro, Black Wealth/White Wealth: A New Perspective on Racial Inequality, 169 (wealth transfers matter most at the top and bottom of wealth spectrum).

14. Dalton Conley conducted an extensive study of the connection between family transfers and the racial gap in wealth. Conley's study looked at data from several generations to determine how much of the racial wealth gap could be explained by differences in parental net worth. After controlling for income, occupation, age, family structure, education, and a host of other demographic variables that might affect an individual's net worth, Conley found that racial differences in

parental wealth was a significant factor in explaining the wealth gap. Dalton Conley, Being Black, Living in the Red: Race, Wealth and Social Policy in America (1999).

15. Maury Gittleman & Edward N. Wolff, *Racial Differences in Patterns of Wealth Accumulation*, 34 J. Human Res. 193 (2004).

16. Kirk White, *Initial Conditions at Emancipation: The Long-Run Effect on Black-White Wealth and Earnings Inequality*, 31 J. Econ. Dyn. & Cont. 3370 (2007).

17. Conley, Being Black, Living in the Red: Race, Wealth and Social Policy in America, *supra* note 174, at 34 (recounting the detailed history of the failure of land redistribution after the Civil War).

18. Laura E. Gómez, Manifest Destinies: The Making of the Mexican American Race (2007).

19. Erik Hurst et al., *The Wealth Dynamics of American Families, 1984–94*, 1 Brookings Papers on Econ. Activity 267 (1998).

20. Robert R. Callis & Melissa Kresin, *U.S. Census Bureau News,: Residential Vacancies and Homeownership in the Fourth Quarter of 2011*, US Dep't of Commerce (Jan. 31, 2012).

21. Kerwin Kofi Charles & Erik Hurst, *The Transition to Home Ownership and the Black-White Wealth Gap*, 84 Rev. of Econ. & Stat. 281, 295 (2002). Thomas Shapiro estimates that 46 percent of whites get assistance in some form, versus 12 percent of black families. Shapiro, The Hidden Cost of Being African American, 112.

22. Charles & Hurst, *The Transition to Home Ownership and the Black-White Wealth Gap*, 295.

23. Oliver & Shapiro, Black Wealth/White Wealth: A New Perspective on Racial Inequality, 148.

24. Thomas Shapiro & Heather Johnson, Symposium, *Assets, Race, and Educational Choices, in Inclusion in Asset Building: Research and Policy Symposium* 10 (2000).

25. Conley, Being Black, Living in the Red: Race, Wealth and Social Policy in America.

26. Dalton Conley, *Capital for College: Parental Assets and Postsecondary Schooling*, 74 Soc. of Educ. 59, 66–68 (2001) (reporting an advantage of .23 to .32 years of schooling). *See also* Conley, Being Black, Living in the Red: Race, Wealth and Social Policy in America, 68 (reporting the same result for high school attendance and completion).

27. *Is College Worth It? College Presidents and Public Assess Value, Quality, Mission of Higher Education*, Pew Res. Ctr. 6–7 (May 16, 2011).

28. Miles Corak & Patrizio Piraino, *The Intergenerational Transmission of Employers*, 29 J. Labor Econ. 37 (2011).

29. *Id.* 45.

30. *Id.* at 48–49.

31. *Id.* at 48–49.

32. *Id.* at 45–46.

33. *Id.* at 53.

34. Tom Hertz, *Rags, Riches, and Race: The Intergenerational Economic Mobility of Black and White Families in the United States, in* Unequal Chances: Family Background and Economic Success 165 (Samuel Bowles et al. eds., 2008).

35. Bowles, Samuel and Herbert Gintis, *The Inheritance of Inequality*, 16 J. of Econ. Perspectives 3–30 (2002). Bowles and Gintis argue that transmission from parent to child is far from perfect.

NOTES TO CHAPTER 5

1. Jerome Karabel, The Chosen: The Hidden History of Admission and Exclusion at Harvard, Yale, and Princeton (2005).

2. *Id.* at 192.

3. *Id.* at 192–94. *See also* Dennis L Gilbert, The American Class Structure in an Age of Growing Inequality 150–53 (2008).

4. As David Luban points out, the rules of baseball (literally the rules of the game) are officially written down and sanctioned by potential prescribed punishment or exclusion from competition, but are also supplemented with an informal "code of the street" set of rules, including a rule prohibiting batters from looking back to see what signals a catcher might be sending the pitcher. The informal norm permits pitchers to strike the batter who violates this rule with the ball, and referees frequently look the other way when this happens. David Luban, *The Inevitability of Conscience: A Response to My Critics*, 93 Cornell L. Rev. 1437, 1441–42 (2008).

5. Drawing on Brian Arthur's work in high-tech markets, Douglass North has argued that institutional rules trigger similar kinds of increasing returns for the reasons that Arthur describes in connection with high tech markets. The following discussion tracks the North-Arthur outline. Douglass C. North, Institutions, Institutional Change and Economic Performance (1990).

6. Douglass C. North, Economic Performance Through Time, Nobel Prize Lecture (Dec. 9, 1993) *in* 8 Am. Econ. Rev. 359 (1994).

7. *See* W. Brian Arthur, *Competing Technologies, Increasing Returns and Lock-In by Historical Events*, 99 Econ. J. 116 (1989). Others have criticized this story of lock-in, arguing that real differences in technological superiority justified the outcome. *See* Stan J. Liebowitz & Stephen E. Margolis, *Path Dependence, Lock-in, and History*, 11 J. Law Econ. & Org. 205 (1995).

8. *See* Benjamin Schneider, *The People Make the Place*, 40 Personnel Psych. 437 (1987); *see also* The People Make the Place: Dynamic Linkages Between Individuals and Organizations (D. Brent Smith ed., 2008); Benjamin Schneider et al., *The ASA Framework: An Update*, 48 Personnel Psych. 747 (1995).

9. Affirmative Action for the Rich: Legacy Preferences in College Admissions (Richard Kahlenberg ed., 2010).

10. *See* Thomas J. Espenshade & Chan Y. Chung, *The Opportunity Cost of Admissions Preferences at Elite Universities*, 86 Soc. Sci. Q. 293, 293 (2005).

11. Chad Coffman, et al., *An Empirical Analysis of Legacy Preferences on Alumni Giving at Top Universities, in* Affirmative Action for the Rich.

12. Richard D. Kahlenberg, *Ten Myths About Legacy Preferences in College Admissions,* The Chronicle of Higher Education (Sept. 22, 2010).

13. *Id. See also* Affirmative Action for the Rich.

14. Karabel, The Chosen: The Hidden History of Admission and Exclusion at Harvard, Yale, and Princeton.

15. *See* Gould, The Mismeasure of Man.

16. Julius Goebel, Jr., A History of the School of Law: Columbia University 337 (1955).

17. A History of the School of Law, Columbia University 337 (Julius Goebel, Jr. ed., 1955). *See also* Eulius Simien, *The Law School Admission Test as a Barrier to Almost Twenty Years of Affirmative Action*, 12 T. Marshall L. Rev. 359, 373–74 (1987); Thomas O. White, *LSAT/LSAS: A Brief History*, 34 J. Legal Educ. 369 (1984).

18. William LaPiana, *Merit and Diversity: The Origins of the Law School Admissions Test*, 48 St. Louis U. L. J. 955 (2003–04).

19. *Id.*

20. Jerold S. Auerbach, Unequal Justice: Lawyers and Social Change in Modern America (Oxford Univ. Press, 1976). *See also* Richard L. Abel, American Lawyers (1989); Daria Roithmayr, *Deconstructing the Distinction Between Merit and Bias*, 85 Cal. L. Rev. 1449 (1997).

21. Brief for Respondents at 4, *Gratz v. Bollinger*, 539 US 244 (2003) (No. 02-516).

22. Susan P. Dalessandro et al., *LSAT Performance with Regional, Gender, and Racial/Ethnic Breakdowns: 2003–2004 Through 2009–2010 Testing Years*, LSAT Technical Report Series (2010). *See* similar reports issued in 2001, 2003, and earlier years.

23. *See e.g.*, William Kidder, *Rise of the Testocracy: An Essay on the LSAT, Conventional Wisdom and the Dismantling of Diversity*, 5 Tex. J. of Women and Law 167 (1999–2000).

24. *See* David Goldberg, Racist Culture: Philosophy and the Politics of Meaning 15–40 (1993).

25. Karen Sloan, Possibility of a Voluntary LSAT Reignites Debate over Test's Value, National Law Journal, Feb. 1, 2011.

26. Arthur T. Denzau & Douglass C. North, *Shared Mental Models: Ideologies and Institutions*, 47 Kyklos 3 (1994).

27. Kathleen Thelen, How Institutions Evolve : The Political Economy of Skills in Germany, Britain, the United States and Japan (2004) (describing structuralist notions of positive feedback in political economy theories of change and persistence).

28. Johnson v. McIntosh, 21 US 543 (1823).

29. *Id.*

NOTES TO CHAPTER 6

1. *See* Deirdre A. Royster, Race and the Invisible Hand: How White Networks Exclude Black Men from Blue-Collar Jobs (2003).

2. *See* Robert D. Putnam, Bowling Alone: The Collapse and Revival of American Community (2001).

3. Pierre Bourdieu & Loïc J. D. Wacquant, An Invitation to Reflexive Sociology (1992).

4. Kaivan Munshi, *Networks in the Modern Economy: Mexican Migrants in the U.S. Labor Market*, 118 Q. J. Econ. 549 (2003).

5. Antoni Calvó-Armengol, *Job Contact Networks*, 115 J. Econ. Theory 191 (2004).

6. Lisa Finneran & Morgan Kelly, *Social Networks and Inequality*, 53 J. Urb. Econ. 282 (2003).

7. Mark S. Granovetter, *The Strength of Weak Ties*, 78 Am. J. Soc. 1360 (1973). *See also* Mark S. Granovetter, Getting a Job: A Study of Contacts and Careers (1995).

8. Nan Lin et al., *Social Resources and Strength of Ties: Structural Factors in Occupational Status Attainment*, 46 Am. Sociol. Rev. 393 (1981).

9. Granovetter, Getting a Job: A Study of Contacts and Careers, 52.

10. Ronald S. Burt, Structural Holes: The Social Structure of Competition (1995). Structural holes can create a competitive advantage for a person whose relationships bridge the holes or gaps. Holes provide this individual an opportunity to control the flow of information between the disconnected parts of the network. Nan Lin, Social Capital: A Theory of Social Structure and Action 70–71 (2001).

11. Alejandro Portes, *Social Capital: Its Origins and Applications in Modern Sociology*, 24 Ann. Rev. Sociol. 1, 3–4 (1998).

12. Granovetter, *The Strength of Weak Ties*, 1371. *See also* Granovetter, Getting a Job: A Study of Contacts and Careers. Granovetter's work documents that the percentage of jobs located via network referral is lower for blacks than for whites.

13. *See* Roger Waldinger & Michael I. Lichter, *Network, Bureaucracy, and Exclusion in* How the Other Half Works: Immigration and the Social Organization of Labor 83–99 (2003).

14. David S. Wilson, *Gossip and Other Aspects of Language as Group-Level Adaptations, in* Cognition and Evolution 347–63 (Cecilia M. Heyes & Ludwig Huber eds., 2000).

15. Sociologist Pierre Bourdieu defines social capital as the pool of actual or potential resources that are linked to membership in a network of acquaintance or recognition. Pierre Bourdieu, *The Forms of Capital, in* Handbook of Theory and Research for the Sociology of Education 248 (J.G. Richardson ed., 1985).

16. Lin, Social Capital: A Theory of Social Structure and Action.

17. Antoni Calvó-Armengol & Matthew O. Jackson, *The Effects of Social Networks on Employment and Inequality*, 94 Am. Econ. Rev. 426 (2004).

18. Loïc J. D. Wacquant & William Julius Wilson, *The Cost of Racial and Class Exclusion in the Inner City*, 501 Ann. AAPSS 8 (1989).

19. William Julius Wilson, The Truly Disadvantaged: The Inner City, the Underclass, and Public Policy (1990).

20. Finneran & Kelly, *Social Networks and Inequality*.

21. Using data from the 1996 General Social Survey, Orlando Patterson finds that blacks have more overlap in their social connections when compared to whites. Orlando Patterson, Rituals of Blood: Consequences of Slavery in Two American Centuries (1998).

22. James D. Montgomery, *Social Networks and Labor-Market Outcomes: Toward an Economic Analysis*, 81 Am. Econ. Rev. 1408 (1991).

23. Kenneth Arrow & Ron Borzekowski, *Limited Network Connections and the Distribution of Wages* 4 (FEDS Working Paper, 2004).

24. *Id.*

25. *See* Lin, Social Capital: A Theory of Social Structure and Action, 66.

26. *See* Yannis M. Ioannides & Linda Datcher Loury, *Job Information Networks, Neighborhood Effects, and Inequality*, 42 J. Econ. Lit. 1056, 1066 (2004).

27. Avner Greif's work on the Maghibri traders is most well-known. Avner Greif, Institutions and the Path to the Modern Economy: Lessons From Medieval Trade (2006).

28. Troy Tassier & Filippo Menczer, *Social Network Structure, Segregation, and Equality in a Labor Market with Referral Hiring*, 66 J. Econ Behav. & Org. 514 (2008).

29. Ioannides & Loury, *Job Information Networks, Neighborhood Effects, and Inequality*.

NOTES TO CHAPTER 7

1. Roland Bénabou, *Equity and Efficiency in Human Capital Investment: The Local Connection*, 63 Rev. of Econ. Stud. 237, 238–39 (1996). *See also* Roland Bénabou, *Human Capital, Inequality, and Growth: A Local Perspective*, 38 Eur. Econ. Rev. 817 (1994).

2. *See* Dennis Epple & Richard Romano, *Competition Between Private and Public Schools, Vouchers, and Peer-Group Effects*, 88 Am. Econ. Rev. 33 (1998); Raquel Fernandez & Richard Rogerson, *Income Distribution, Communities, and the Quality of Public Education*, 111 Q. J. Econ. 135 (1996).

3. Beyond the self-reinforcing advantage to whites that historical monopoly conferred, blacks also suffered accompanying disadvantage in their ability to pay for housing in segregated neighborhoods. According to historian Arnold Hirsch, blacks paid more to buy housing in segregated neighborhoods, largely because supply was restricted to a smaller geographic space. At least in the rental market, blacks paid 15 to 50 percent higher rent than whites paid for similar accommodations. Arnold Hirsch, Making the Second Ghetto: Race & Housing in Chicago 1940–1960, at 29 (1983).

4. Bénabou, *Equity and Efficiency in Human Capital Investment*, 257–58.

5. 557 US 701 (2007).

6. Thomas C. Schelling, Micromotives and Macrobehavior (1978).

7. Paul Krugman, *History and Industry Location: The Case of the Manufacturing Belt*, 81 Am. Econ. Rev. 80 (1991); Arthur, *Increasing Returns and Path Dependence in the Economy*, 49–67.

8. Robert J. Sampson & Patrick Sharkey, *Neighborhood Selection and the Social Reproduction of Concentrated Racial Inequality*, 45 Demography 1 (2008).

9. *Id.* at 15.

10. *Id.* at 16; *id.* at 17. These kinds of studies are notoriously difficult because of something called the "selection bias" problem. Looking at the effect of changing neighborhoods was difficult because the studies were collecting data from a very special group of people—those who chose to move—and not from a random cross-section of research subjects. This was potentially a problem because some omitted variable—like the movers' ambition—might explain the benefits or losses associated with moving to a new neighborhood, and not the neighborhood itself. Sampson and Sharkey solved this problem in two ways. First, they widened their lens to study the neighborhoods themselves, by keeping track of both the movers—those who moved in and those who moved out, and the stayers—the city residents who stayed behind, a group that made up a majority of those studied. The authors also followed up on the outmovers who left Chicago, to see how they did when they moved somewhere else. *Id.* at 2.

11. For a review of the research, *see* Xavier de Souza Briggs & Margery Austin Turner, *Assisted Housing Mobility and the Success of Low-Income Minority Families: Lessons for Policy, Practice, and Future Research*, 1 Nw. J. Law & Soc. Pol'y 25 (2006).

12. Patrick Sharkey, *The Intergenerational Transmission of Context*, 113 Am. J. Soc. 931 (2008).

13. *Id.* at 933.

14. Jeanne Brooks-Gunn et al., Neighborhood Poverty: Context and Consequences for Children 110 (1997).

15. Albert Saiz & Susan Wachter, *Immigration and the Neighborhood*, 3 Am. Econ. J. Econ. Pol'y 169 (2011).

16. Kenneth T. Jackson, Crabgrass Frontier: The Suburbanization of the United States (1985).

17. William Julius Wilson, More Than Just Race: Being Black and Poor in the Inner City; Jackson, Crabgrass Frontier.

18. Michael A. Stoll, *Within Cities and Suburbs: Racial Residential Concentration and the Spatial Distribution of Employment Opportunities across Submetropolitan Areas*, 19 J. Pol'y Analysis & Mgmt. 207, 227–29 (2000). *See also* Roger D. Waldinger, Ethnic Los Angeles 38 (1996); Christopher Jencks & Susan E. Mayer, *Residential Segregation, Job Proximity, and Black Job Opportunities, in* Inner-City Poverty in the United States 187–88 (Laurence E. Lynn & Michael G.H. McGeary eds., 1990).

19. *See* Sheryll Cashin, The Failures of Integration: How Race and Class Are Undermining the American Dream (2004).

20. Mary Patillo-McCoy, Black Picket Fences: Privilege and Peril Among the Black Middle-Class (1999).

21. *See* Loïc J. D. Wacquant, Urban Outcasts: A Comparative Sociology of Advanced Marginality (2007).

22. *Id.*

23. Wilson, More Than Just Race: Being Black and Poor in the Inner City.

24. Wilson, The Truly Disadvantaged: The Inner-City, the Underclass, and Public Policy. Douglas Massey and Mitchell Eggers have challenged Wilson's hypothesis, with empirical data indicating little correlation between the increases in segregation based on class and increased isolation of nonwhite neighborhoods. Douglas S. Massey & Mitchell L. Eggers, *The Ecology of Inequality: Minorities and the Concentration of Poverty, 1970–1980*, 95 Am. J. Sociol. 1153 (1990). Wilson has responded that because nonpoor blacks often move into neighborhoods with smaller but still significant levels of poverty, the indices for interclass segregation are not sufficiently informative about the impact on the neighborhood left behind. William Julius Wilson, *Studying Inner-City Dislocations: The Challenge of Public Agenda Research*, 56 Am. J. Sociol. 1 (1991).

25. *See* Richard Ford, *The Boundaries of Race: Political Geography in Legal Analysis*, 107 Harv. L. Rev. 1841 (1994).

26. Ron Zimmer & John T. Jones, *Unintended Consequence of Centralized Public School Funding in Michigan Education*, 71 So. Econ. J. 534 (2005).

27. Milliken v. Bradley, 418 US 717 (1974).

28. Missouri v. Jenkins, 515 US 70 (1995).

29. Wacquant, Urban Outcasts: A Comparative Sociology of Advanced Marginality, 268.

30. Loïc Wacquant, *Deadly Symbiosis: When Ghetto and Prison Meet and Mesh*, 3 Punishment & Soc'y 95, 96 (2001).

31. *See* Ian Haney López, Post Racial Racism: Racial Stratification and Mass Incarceration in the Age of Obama, 98 Cal. L. Rev. 1023 (2010); Michelle Alexander, The New Jim Crow: Mass Incarceration in the Age of Colorblindness (2010).

32. Christy Fisher and Jill Farrell, Chicago Communities and Prisoner Reentry, Urban Institute Report (September 2005).

33. For an overview of the debate about felon disenfranchisement, *see* Pamela S. Karlan, *Convictions and Doubts: Retribution, Representation, and the Debate over Felon Disenfranchisement*, 56 Stan. L. Rev. 1147 (2004).

NOTES TO CHAPTER 8

1. Robert J. Sampson & Jeffrey D. Morenoff, *Durable Inequality: Spatial Dynamics, Social Processes, and the Persistence of Poverty in Chicago Neighborhoods*, in Poverty Traps 176–203 (Samuel Bowles et al. eds., 2006).

2. The correlation coefficient for neighborhood poverty rankings and rates from 1970 to 1990 was .87. *Id.* at 179.

3. Poverty rates for the average neighborhood studied increased from 11 to 20 percent. *Id.* at 182.

4. *Id.* at 182.

5. Arthur, *Increasing Returns and Path Dependence in the Economy*.

6. *See* Paul A. David, *Understanding the Economics of QWERTY: The Necessity of History*, in Economic History and Modern Economics 30–49 (William N. Parker ed., 1986). *See also* Paul A. David, Why Are Institutions the 'Carriers of History?'

Notes on Path-Dependence and the Evolution of Conventions, Organizations and Institutions, 5 Struct. Changes & Econ. Dyn. 205 (1994); Paul A. David, *Clio and the Economics of QWERTY*, 75 Am. Econ. Rev. 332, 332–34 (1985). For an argument against QWERTY as an example of path-dependence, *see* Liebowitz & Margolis, Winners, Losers & Microsoft: Competition and Antitrust in High Technology.

7. Scott Page has argued that the relative disadvantage or "negative externalities" created by the QWERTY feedback loop are the primary cause of path dependence. Scott E. Page, An Essay on the Existence and Causes of Path Dependence, 29–31 (unpublished essay, Univ. of Michigan) (on file with author). In my view, Page's argument confuses the issue. First, it is the positive feedback loop—positive in the sense not that it confers benefits but that it produces movement in the same direction—that creates both positive and negative externalities. Second, I would argue that in most real-world cases, both the negative externalities experienced by competitor keyboards and the positive externalities enjoyed by QWERTY are incident to the same institutional feedback loop. To be sure, in the theoretical world, feedback loops could create positive externalities or effects—effects that benefit one competitor—without creating negative effects on competitors. But practically speaking, in a world of limited resources, any feedback loop that confers positive benefits on a dominant market player is likely also to confer negative effects on competitors in the same market.

8. David, *Clio and the Economics of QWERTY. See also* David, Understanding the Economics of QWERTY: The Necessity of History (responding to the Liebowitz and Margolis critique).

9. Actually, to be a bit more precise, the probability of the draw doesn't have to be exactly equal to the proportion in the urn—it can be a looser function of the proportion in the urn.

10. Arthur uses the Polya urn mathematical model to explain the concept of lock-in. Arthur, *Increasing Returns and Path Dependence*, 36–38. As Arthur notes, the Polya urn model is too restrictive for most types of path-dependence and lock-in. The model is particularly restrictive because it requires that the probability of a particular colored ball on subsequent draws be exactly equal to the proportion of the balls of that color already contained in the urn. For most path-dependent processes, the likelihood of subsequent events operates as a more general function of past events—the probability of adding a red ball is a function of the proportion of red balls already in the urn. Arthur and his colleagues have developed alternative mathematical models to expand the application of the Polya model, and have adapted their model to accommodate more than one color and probability functions that change over time. *See id.* at 38.

11. *Id.* at 40, 44.

12. Joseph Farrell & Paul Klemperer, *Coordination and Lock-in: Competition with Switching Costs and Network Effects, in* Handbook of Industrial Organization 1967, 1977 (Mark Armstrong & Robert H. Porter eds., 2007)

13. William Greider, The Education of David Stockman, The Atlantic 141 (December 1981).

14. Bénabou, *Equity and Efficiency in Human Capital Investment*.

15. Because capital markets are imperfect, differences in wealth will pose significant obstacles for poorer nonwhites to switch neighborhoods. *See* Michael H. Schill & Susan M. Wachter, *Housing Market Constraints and Spatial Stratification by Income and Race*, 6 Housing Pol'y Debate 141, 145–46 (1995).

16. Bénabou, *Equity and Efficiency in Human Capital Investment*.

17. Arthur, *Increasing Returns*, 10.

18. *See* Brian J. L. Berry, Islands of Renewal in Seas of Decay in The New Urban Reality (Paul E. Peterson ed., 1985).

19. *See* Peter Marcuse, *Gentrification, Abandonment, and Displacement: Connections, Causes, and Policy Responses in New York City*, 28 J. Urb. Contemp. L. 195 (1985).

20. *See* Daria Roithmayr, *Barriers to Entry: A Market Lock-In Model of Discrimination*, 86 Va. L. Rev. 727, 776–78 (2000).

21. The correlation coefficient of the LSAT to first year grade averages is roughly .39, which means that the LSAT explains approximately 16 percent of the variation in first-year grades. This coefficient is substantially lower for LSAT scores in the twenty-fifth percentile (.34) than for 50th (.40) or 75th (.44). Andrea E. Thornton et. al., Predictive Validity of the LSAT: A National Summary of the 1999–2000 Correlation Studies, LSAC Research Report Series, Technical Report 01-025 (December 2005). Lest this cost of lost predictive ability assume too much importance, one should consider that the choice of what qualities are important in law students and in the legal profession was itself produced, at least at the outset, by exclusively white men in the legal market.

22. Robert Morse & Sam Flanigan, *Methodology: Law School Rankings*, US News (Mar. 12, 2012).

23. Willis Reese, *The Standard Law School Admission Test*, 1 J. Legal Ed. 124, 124–25 (1948).

24. Daria Roithmayr, *Barriers to Entry*.

25. William A. Fischel, The Homevoter Hypothesis: How Home Values Influence Government Taxation, School Finance, and Land-Use Policies (2001).

26. Serrano v. Priest (Serrano II), 18 Cal. 3d 728 (1976) (the Court in Serrano II confirmed that the California constitution rendered disparate funding unconstitutional, preserving the Serrano I ruling despite a finding that in another Supreme Court case, the Fourteenth Amendment is not violated by disparate funding); Serrano v. Priest (Serrano I), 5 Cal. 3d 584 (1971).

27. *See* Fischel, The Homevoter Hypothesis, 99–100.

28. For an excellent overview of the Micawber threshold and poverty traps, *see* Michael R. Carter & Christopher B. Barrett, *The Economics of Poverty Traps and Persistent Poverty: An Asset-based Approach*, 42 J. Dev. Stud. 178 (2006). For more information on poverty traps, *see also* Poverty Traps, (Bowles et al. eds., 2006);

Costas Azariadis, *The Economics of Poverty Traps, Part One: Complete Markets*, 1 J. Econ. Growth 449 (1996).

29. Dalton Conley & Rebecca Glauber, Black-White Differences in Income and Wealth Mobility 9–13 (Jan. 2007) (paper presented to the Sixth Meeting of the University Working Groups on the Social Dimensions of Inequality, sponsored by the Russell Sage Foundation and the Carnegie Corporation).

30. Michelle Adato, et al., *Exploring Poverty Traps and Social Exclusion in South Africa Using Qualitative and Quantitative Data*, 42 J. Dev. Stud. 226, 244 (1996).

31. Finneran & Kelly, Social Networks and Inequality, 293. *See also* Morgan Kelly, *The Dynamics of Smithian Growth*, 112 Q. J. Econ. 939 (1997) (arguing that below a critical threshold level of transportation networks, markets remain isolated and specialized, and above the threshold, markets fuse in a large economy and growth accelerates exponentially).

32. Michele Boldrin, *Public Education and Capital Accumulation*, 59 Res. in Econ. 85 (2005) (arguing that public financing solves a free-rider problem in economies in which markets for financing educational investment are incomplete).

NOTES TO CHAPTER 9

1. 488 US 469 (1989).

2. *Id.* at 469.

3. *Id.* at 499.

4. Brief of Appellant City of Richmond, at 22, City of Richmond v. J.A. Croson Co., 488 US 469 (1989) (No. 87-998).

5. *Id.* at 4.

6. *Croson*, 488 US at 469–70.

7. *Id.* at 499–501, 503.

8. Brief Amicus Curiae for the NAACP Legal Defense & Education Fund, Inc., at 38–40, City of Richmond v. J.A. Croson, Co., 488 US 469 (1989) (No. 87-998).

9. Scott Page correctly points out that increasing returns do not necessarily lead to path-dependence, monopoly or to lock-in. In the event that two or more technologies can take advantage of increasing returns at roughly the same rate, then those technologies may remain competitive with one another, and small historical events will not necessarily affect market outcomes. Page, An Essay on the Existence and Causes of Path Dependence.

10. Abigail Thernstrom & Stephan Thernstrom, No Excuses: Closing the Racial Gap in Learning (2004).

11. *Croson*, 488 US at 503.

12. *See* Oliver & Shapiro, Black Wealth/White Wealth: A New Perspective on Racial Inequality, 109–10.

13. Thernstrom & Thernstrom, No Excuses: Closing the Racial Gap in Learning; *see generally* Camille Z. Charles, *Racial Inequality and College Attendance: The Mediating Role of Parental Investments*, 36 Soc. Sci. Res. 329 (2007); David Mechanic

& Jennifer Tanner, *Vulnerable People, Groups, and Populations: Societal View*, 26 Health Aff. 1220 (2007); Amy L. Wax, *Engines of Inequality: Class, Race, and Family Structure*, 41 Fam. L.Q. 567 (2007).

14. Stephen Jay Gould, Wonderful Life: The Burgess Shale and the Nature of History 277–78, 280 (1989) (arguing that contingent events like the collision of an asteroid with the earth determine the path of evolution).

15. Ford, *The Boundaries of Race: Political Geography in Legal Analysis* 293.

16. Kousser, The Shaping of Southern Politics 236–37.

17. W. Brian Arthur, *Process and Emergence in the Economy, in* The Economy as an Evolving Complex System II (W. Brian Arthur et al. eds., 1997).

18. Becker, The Economics of Discrimination; John J. Donohue, *Is Title VII Efficient?*, 134 U. Pa. L. Rev. 1411 (1986); *see* Richard Posner, *The Efficiency and Efficacy of Title VII*, 136 U. Pa. L. Rev. 513 (1987).

19. Michael A. Cusumano et al., *Strategic Maneuvering and Mass-Market Dynamics: The Triumph of VHS over Beta*, 66 Bus. Hist. Rev. 51 (1992); *see also* Arthur, Increasing Returns and Path Dependence in the Economy; W. Brian Arthur, *Positive Feedbacks in the Economy*, Scientific American, Feb. 1990, at 92.

20. Arthur, Increasing Returns and Path Dependence in the Economy 112.

21. *See generally* Ronald Bénabou, *Workings of a City: Location, Education, and Production*, 108 Q. J. Econ. 619 (1993).

22. *Id.* at 639, 649.

23. David M. Cutler & Edward L. Glaeser, *Are Ghettos Good or Bad?* 112 Q. J. Econ. 827 (1997).

24. Samuel Bowles & Rajiv Sethi, *Social Segregation and the Dynamics of Group Inequality* 14–15 (Univ. of Mass. Amherst Econ. Dep't Working Paper Series, Paper 56, 2006).

25. Robert D. Putnam, *E Pluribus Unum: Diversity and Community in the Twenty-first Century*, 30 Scand. Pol. Stud. 137, 149. (2007).

26. *Id.* at 162–64. Research by Tajfel and Turner confirms that creating a common purpose can ameliorate the effect of in-group and out-group bias and lack of trust. In the Robber's Cave experiment, boys who had been assigned randomly to one camp or another displayed both out-group and in-group bias. When researchers asked the boys to come together to solve a common problem, the effects of group bias diminished considerably. H Tajfel & JC Turner, *The Social Identity Theory of Intergroup Behavior in* Psychology of Intergroup Relations (Stephen Worchel & William G. Austin eds., 1986).

27. 579 F. Supp. 574 (N.D. Ill. 1983).

28. *See* Lester C. Thurow, Poverty and Discrimination (1969).

29. In the *Standard Oil* case, the Court ordered the dissolution of the principal holding company, which acted through its subsidiaries to divide up the country into districts for anticompetitive purposes. *See* Std. Oil Co. of N.J. v. United States, 221 US 1 (1911) (holding that unification of power in the hands of one holding

company raises presumption of an intent to exclude and centralize perpetual control). In the *AT&T* case, the court ordered the divestiture of the so-called Baby Bells as part of a consent decree. *See* Maryland v. United States, 460 US 1001 (1983), *aff'g United States v. Am. Tel. & Tel. Co.*, 552 F. Supp. 131 (D.D.C. 1982) (approving consent decree to divest Bell Operating Companies).

30. *Microsoft*, 159 F.R.D. 318.

NOTES TO CHAPTER 10

1. Darrick Hamilton & William Darity, Jr., Can 'Baby Bonds' Eliminate the Racial Wealth Gap in Putative Post-Racial America?" 37 Rev. Black Pol. Econ. 207 (2010).

2. The UK has shut this program down as of 2010. Howard Glennerster, *Why Was a Wealth Tax for the UK Abandoned? Lessons for the Policy Process and Tackling Wealth Inequality*, 41 J. Soc. Pol'y 233 (2012).

3. Robin Cowan & Staffan Hulten, *Escaping Lock-In: The Case of the Electric Vehicle*, 53 Tech. Forecasting & Soc. Change 61 (1996).

4. *Id.*

5. Paul Krugman, *For Richer*, New York Times, Oct. 20, 2002.

6. Roberto Mangabeira Unger, Democracy Realized: The Progressive Alternative 205 (1998).

7. Section 15: Race & Color Discrimination, in EEOC Comp. Man. (2006).

8. Pew Research Center for the People and the Press, American Values Survey 2012, Q 40i.

9. Networks increase in value if they are sufficiently small and exclusive to ensure the value of membership is high, and the value of a recommendation from someone else in the network is high. Research indicates that the cost of screening large amounts of information, whether by the job search applicant or by the employer looking to hire, may limit the usefulness of online networks, so networks should be of some optimum size, both large and small enough to be useful. *See* Christine Fountain, *Finding a Job in the Internet Age*, 83 Soc. Forces 1235 (2005).

10. *See* Stacy Teicher, *Working the Electronic Grapevine*, The Christian Sci. Monitor (Mar. 8, 2004).

11. Steve Hanway, *Minority Teens Less Likely to Socialize Via Web*, Gallup, (June 10, 2003). The poll documents that minority teens spend less time socializing with people they know in their social networks, but more time in chat rooms talking to people they don't know. Researchers speculated that this disparity could be explained by network limitations, where others in the network have relatively less access to the Internet.

12. Three out of five Filipino Americans have Friendster accounts. Ted Reyes, *Friendster: The New Pinoy Phenomenon*, The Filipino Express, July 31, 2005.

13. Stacey Blake-Beard et al., *Unfinished Business: The Impact of Race on Understanding Mentoring Relationships, in* The Handbook of Mentoring at Work: Theory, Research

and Practice (Belle Rose Ragins ed. 2007); David Thomas, *Racial Dynamics in Cross-Race Developmental Relationships*, 38 Admin. Sci. Q. 169 (1993).

14. For example, in Minneapolis, metropolitan areas are required to contribute to a regional pool 40 percent of the growth of the district's commercial industrial tax base acquired after 1971. Minneapolis's regional approach has helped to reduce disparities between wealthy suburban and poor urban areas from 50 to 1 to 12 to 1. Myron Orfield, Metropolitics: A Regional Agenda for Community and Stability 87 (1997).

15. David Rusk, *Inclusionary Zoning: A Key Tool in the Search for Workable Affordable Housing Programs*, 88 Pub. Mgmt. 18, 18–19 (2006).

16. *See* Andrew Dietderich, *An Egalitarian's Market: The Economics of Inclusionary Zoning Reclaimed*, 24 Ford. Urb. L. J. 23 (1996).

17. *See* Nan Lin, *Inequality in Social Capital*, 29 Contemp. Soc. 785, 785–93 (2000); Pierre Bourdieu & Jean-Claude Passeron, Reproduction in Education, Society and Culture (1977).

18. Bruce Ackerman, & Anne Alstott, The Stakeholder Society (1999).

19. Hillary Clinton has proposed baby bonds, which would provide $500 to every child at birth and an additional installment at age 10. Funds could be used for college or vocational training, first-home purchase or retirement planning. Savings Accounts at Birth and Other Children's Savings Accounts Proposals, New Am. Found. (2006). Senators Santorum, Corzine, Schumer, and DeMint, along with Representatives Ford, Kennedy, and English, have proposed a very similar account, except that low-income children could receive a one-time supplemental deposit of up to $500 and would be eligible to receive an additional $500 in matching funds for money voluntarily saved each year.

20. Shapiro et al., The Racial Wealth Gap Increases Fourfold.

21. James E. Rauch, *Black Ties Only? Ethnic Business Networks, Intermediaries, and African American Retail Entrepreneurship, in* Networks and Markets 270 (James Rauch & Alessandra Casella eds., 2001). *See also* James E. Rauch & Alessandra Casella, *Overcoming Informational Barriers to International Resource Allocation: Prices and Group Ties*, 113 Econ. J. 21 (2003) (making a similar argument regarding the use of informational networks by developing countries in international trade).

22. Marta Tienda and Rebeca Raijman argue that informal networks are still superior to formal business organizations, because the formal organizations cannot provide some of the functions served by informal ties. They have suggested that Rauch include links to other retailers and encourage the growth of new businesses that could be vertically integrated with black retailers. Marta Tienda & Rebeca Raijman, *Ethnic Ties and Entrepreneurship: Comment on "Black Ties Only? Ethnic Business Networks, Intermediaries, and African American Retail Entrepreneurship," in* Networks and Markets, 310 (James Rauch & Alessandra Casella eds., 2001).

23. Roberto M. Fernandez & Isabel Fernandez-Mateo, *Networks, Race, and Hiring*, 71 Am. Soc. Rev. 42 (2006).

24. Randal C. Picker, *Simple Games in a Complex World: A Generative Approach to the Adoption of Norms*, 64 U. Chi. L. Rev. 1225, 1228 (1997).

25. For a fascinating discussion of seed clusters and the end of Chinese footbinding, *see* Gerry Mackie, *Ending Footbinding and Infibulation: A Convention Account*, 61 Am. Soc. Rev. 999, 1000–02 (1996).

26. Rosabeth Moss Kanter, Men and Women of the Corporation 211–36 (1977).

27. Sec'y v. Mountain Side Mobile Estates (HUDALJ 08-92-0010-1) (Dec. 17, 1993), 1993 WL 533084 (a secretarial order holding that 1991 amendments implicitly apply to Title VIII to restore disparate impact doctrine after the Supreme Court decision in Wards Cove).

28. Thompson v. US Dep't. of HUD, 220 F. 3d 241 (4th Cir. 2000).

29. Croson 488 US 469 (1989). *See also* Concrete Works of Colo. Inc. v. City and County of Denver, 540 US 1027 (2003) (Scalia, J., dissenting from denial of cert.) (Justice Scalia argues that if size and experience of a firm were held to be impermissible explanations of racial disparity, every field of industry would be affected, and courts could impose no logical stopping point to race-conscious remedies.)

30. *See* Croson, 488 US at 498 (expressing the fear that race-conscious remedies for societal discrimination would "ha[ve] no logical stopping point. . . . 'Relief' for such an ill-defined wrong [societal discrimination] could extend until the percentage of public contracts awarded to MBE's in Richmond mirrored the percentage of minorities in the population as a whole"). *Id.* at 505–06.

31. *Id.* at 474, 485. Likewise, in Wygant v. Jackson Bd. of Educ., 476 US 267 (1995) the Court held that a teacher layoff provision that granted preferences for minority teachers could not be upheld, even where necessary to provide minority role models to children, because societal discrimination had caused the minority underrepresentation on public school faculties. In Wygant, as in preceding case law, the Court assumed that, in the absence of discrimination by the school board, "nondiscriminatory hiring practices will in time result in a workforce more or less representative of the racial and ethnic composition of the population in the community from which employees are hired." *Id.* at 275. The Court went on to say that, although it did not doubt serious historical racial discrimination in the US, remedying societal discrimination was too amorphous and insufficient an interest to justify remedies that burdened innocent people on the basis of their race. *Id.* at 276.

32. Grutter v. Bollinger, 539 US 306 (2003). Parents Involved v. Seattle Sch., 551 US 701 (2007).

NOTES TO THE CONCLUSION

1. Jesus Hernandez, *Redlining Revisited, Mortgage Lending Patterns in Sacramento 1930–2004*, 33 Int'l J. Urb. and Reg'l Res. 291 (2009).

2. Hernandez, *Redlining Revisited*.

ABOUT THE AUTHOR

Daria Roithmayr is the George T. and Harriet E. Pfleger Professor of Law at the University of Southern California Gould School of Law. An internationally acclaimed legal scholar and activist, she is the country's leading voice on the legal analysis of structural racial inequality. Prior to joining USC, Professor Roithmayr served on the faculty at the University of Illinois and advised Senator Edward Kennedy on the nominations of Clarence Thomas and David Souter.